CHINA: A Yellow Peril?
Western relationships with China

RICHARD MUIRHEAD

Typeset by Jonathan Downes,
Cover and Layout by I am Curious Oranj for CFZ Communications
Using Microsoft Word 2000, Microsoft , Publisher 2000, Adobe Photoshop CS.

Photographs © 2009 CFZ except where noted

First published in Great Britain by CFZ Press

CFZ Press
Myrtle Cottage
Woolsery
Bideford
North Devon
EX39 5QR

© CFZ MMIX

All rights reserved. Without limiting the rights under copyright reserved above, no part of this publication may be reproduced, stored in or introduced into a retrieval system, or transmitted, in any form of by any means (electronic, mechanical, photocopying, recording or otherwise), without the prior written permission of both the copyright owners and the publishers of this book.

ISBN: 978-1-905723-41-6

This book is dedicated to my father

Stuart W. Muirhead

(1931-1993)

And

My family

French political cartoon from the late 1890s. A pie represents "Chine" (French for China) and is being divided between UK, Germany, Russia, France and Japan.

Contents

Chapter 1   Introduction

Chapter 2   China's relationship with the West, 1600-1900

Chapter 3   The nemesis of China's isolation: The Boxer Uprising

Chapter 4   Orientalist theories and British imperialism in China

Chapter 5   The Yellow Peril. The Chinese as a threat

Chapter 6   The Yellow Peril scare in The United States

Chapter 7   Chinese Indentured Labour in South Africa

Chapter 8   The Red Peril: The British and the rise of Communism in China

Chapter 9   Conclusion.

Canton Street, in Macclesfield, was named during the Opium Wars of the mid-19th Century. This street is one minute's walk from the author's home, and symbolises the complex links between two cultures.

CHAPTER ONE: INTRODUCTION

This book examines the relationship between China and Britain, between the late Eighteenth and the early Twentieth Centuries. Where it is relevant, those other countries which had an impact upon the course of events in China, and have been influenced by events *in* China before, and during, and after, this time, are also included. There is a particular emphasis on the British, because of the ease of access to relevant archives and the special case of Hong Kong, with Chinese and British living in close proximity, longer than in any other of the British colonies and possessions in the Far East, such as Singapore and Wei-hai-wei.

In order to investigate the hypothesis; that there was a significant degree of interaction between the Chinese and the British, it is necessary to understand how the West became involved in China in the first place. Several questions are addressed: These questions arise from three suggestions related to the primary and secondary material collected and studied during preparation for this work. They are:

- Firstly, what were the implications of the fact that some non-Chinese commentators considered China to be a civilization, whilst others believed it to be a barbarian kingdom?
- Secondly, the ambiguity and confusion in British thinking will be exposed by looking at the hypocrisy in the British posture, for example in condemning the Chinese for practices and behaviour the British also practised, such as opium smoking. The British writers Thomas de Quincey, and Coleridge, whose poem `Xanadu` was allegedly inspired whilst he smoked opium, for example. There were Chinese who smoked opium for leisure during the Victorian era. There was also a certain level of British cynicism; especially about the motives of Chinese politicians and activists with regards to their opposition to the West. There is also the question of whether there was more substance to the `Yellow Peril` scare than just pictorial and verbal imagery.
- Thirdly, were there any positive images? If so, what were they, and what are the implications for *our* understanding of British behaviour towards the Chinese in the late nineteenth and early twen-

tieth centuries? It was found difficult to locate positive images of China, except from Jesuit sources such as Du Halde in the early eighteenth century.

Chapter Two discusses `China's relationship with the West, 1600-1900`. The former country used her skills in metallurgy and astronomy to try to serve the state and people. These skills were superior to Western skills in similar fields, at times reaching a peak several hundred years before the West. This craftsmanship could be seen as a hallmark of a civilized power which, however, was no match for British military power in the early 1840s and late 1850s, when the two Opium Wars took place. The Opium Wars represented a clash between aggressively mercantilist British traders, and an intensely conservative Chinese government.

The beliefs of two Hong Kong governors are then examined to see what impact these convictions had upon the course of events in Hong Kong. These men are Sir John Bowring, governor from 1854-1859, and Sir John Pope-Hennessy, governor from 1877-1882. They are chosen for study because of the interesting and sometimes controversial nature of their policies and, in the case of Pope-Hennessy, the positive response from the local Chinese population to these policies.

Chapter Three is entitled `The nemesis of China's Isolation: The Boxer Uprising.` This reflects the fact that the Boxer Uprising was an act of retributive judgement on two counts. Firstly upon China's own head for trying to throw off the yoke of the West and Japan, a combination far more powerful than itself. Secondly, upon the West and Japan for their oppressive presence in China. The failure of the Uprising to throw out the foreigner seemed to lead to an even greater degree of foreign intervention than beforehand. A summary of the main events of the Boxer Uprising is given and the comments of a Hong Kong-based missionary on events further north are included. These comments were gleaned from letters on microfiche held in the archives of the Methodist Missionary Society at the School of Oriental and African Studies library in London.

In Chapter Four, Edward Said`s Orientalist theories will be considered; in order to ascertain their contribution to the debate on the relationship between China and Britain. These theories will be explained. It is felt that it would be irrelevant to undertake an in-depth discussion of all Orientalist theories in this work. What is pertinent here, is the historical flow of events and the attitudes of British authors, politicians, military men and others to the Chinese. Said`s interpretation (if applied to China) of an all-embracing culture of knowledge by British authors who experienced China, is examined. The Orient is seen by Said through a lens, which looks on this part of the world as serving the imperialist interests of the Occident. The works of Edward Said, particularly his books Orientalism and Culture and Imperialism; have had a great impact on the whole debate. Said`s tendency towards a grand theory of Orientalism has been criticised by John Mackenzie who will be featured in this study. Said`s basic premise is that the policy interests of Western imperialist politicians, in relation to the countries they colonized in the East, were advanced, because the East was portrayed in certain ways which made colonisation easier. This intrusion itself generated a large body of Orientalist texts, as the Orientalists turned the weakness of those in the East into an excuse for colonisation.

The approximate core period 1793 to 1926 has been chosen for study, because of the dramatic events which took place between those dates.

These events held the attention of Western politicians to the extent that they mobilised military and political power, and these interventions helped in varying degrees to influence the presentation of images of the Chinese. These events included the anti-foreign unrest in Hong Kong, 1884, which was sparked off as a result of French expansionism in China; the Sino-Japanese War of 1895, caused by China coming to the defence of Korea when the latter was faced with Japanese militarism; the ceding of the New Territories to Britain in 1898, when they became part of Hong Kong ; and the Boxer Uprising in 1900. At this point the Chinese were most directly a peril to Westerners' lives and property, and Japan distinguished herself, by coming out on the side of the West against the Boxers. The Russo-Japanese War in 1905, saw an Oriental power defeated a Western one, which led some commentators to fear a Chinese - Japanese alliance which would sweep across Eurasia. The Times of January 7th 1905 pointed out, however, that 'the all-powerful Chinese bureaucracy' had a hostility to 'all the ideas of reform which are bound up with Japanese influence', [1] thus making a common alliance unlikely.

The Hong Kong-Canton strike-boycott of 1925-26 is also considered. All of these events, contributed towards the negative image of China; in the minds of Western politicians of those days. That is to say, a China was being presented which was corrupt and which was not capable of looking after its own affairs; so other countries had better do that for China. Photographers, authors, war artists and journalists were also able to present images of China to a wider public. The 'Yellow Peril' scare, possibly originating in Germany in the mid 1890s, sets the idea of China as a barbarian kingdom against the earlier Western idea of China as a civilization.

The main sources used for this chapter, Chapter Five on the 'Yellow Peril' are boys' and girls' comics, national and provincial newspapers for the first decade of the 20th century, and journal and book articles. A problem encountered is the sheer volume of material to assimilate, particularly from the children's comics. The conclusion reached on the 'Yellow Peril' is that it was more of a figment of the imagination than a matter of real substance. There was a great diversity of sources for the origin of the 'Yellow Peril' scare, ranging from fears of Chinese over population to the behaviour of Chinese immigrants in British ports. In Chapter Five all of the above-mentioned international crises are set in the context of the fluctuating social mores and debates, (sometimes intelligent), about the threat of a 'Yellow Peril'. Thanks to Dr John Seed for permission to quote from his web site and reproduce Table 1 from the said site.

(As far as verbal and pictorial imagery is concerned; there is very little change between the 1790s and 1920s in images of Hong Kong. The ubiquitous optimistic harbour photo portrays a bustling port, but does not hint at the darker side, such as conditions for seamen during this time.)

Chapter Six examines the unfortunate position of the Chinese community in the United States when compared with the supremacy of the white working class and ruling class. The Chinese in the United States were in a similar position to their brothers and sisters elsewhere in the West, that is to say, ironically- perilous, they were hardly a Peril themselves. They were treated with contempt by the populace of their host nation, just as they were in Britain, Australia and South Africa, the countries studied in this book. Source material for this chapter includes web sites, non fiction books and a novel.

Chapter Seven examines the case of Chinese indentured labour in South Africa and the special situation there with regards to indentured labour in the aftermath of the Boer War. Thanks to Dr. Karen Harris whose material strongly influenced this chapter. Chapter Eight looks at the early days of communism in China and how this clashed with British imperial interests in Shanghai and Hong Kong, specifically the preservation of free trade. Source material for this chapter included contemporary Hong Kong and Shanghai newspapers held at the British Library Newspaper Library in north London. The problems between the British and Chinese communism arose with the May 30th Movement of students and workers in Shanghai , and were made worse by the lengthy strike of workers in Hong Kong and Canton from 1925 to 1926. The Chinese communist was seen by the British media as 'un-Chinese' because of his pro-Bolshevik leanings. An anomalous instance was the lavish pro-British sentiments expressed by the villagers of Kam Tin in the New Territories of Hong Kong on the return of their village gates from the British in May 1925. Reasons for the 1925-1926 industrial unrest include the significance of this challenge to Western hegemony, by nationalist Chinese workers after so many years of domination by the West.

Chapter Nine, the conclusion, considers the current influence of China in the world, particularly in Africa.

The essential question is, how could the West simultaneously combine an admiration for China, as a great civilisation with policies which would appear to indicate that China was being treated, implicitly or explicitly, with contempt? It must be remembered that `.....attitudes were formed and judgements passed, trade prosecuted and the Gospel preached, against a background of a culture based upon totally different presuppositions from those underlying European culture.` [2] Both pinyin/romanised and original Chinese spellings are given in this text.

Boxer forces in Tianjin during the Boxer Rebellion, also known as the Boxer Uprising, or the Righteous Harmony Society Movement

Fort Victoria, Kowloon

CHAPTER TWO:
China's relationship with the West, 1600-1900

The purpose of this chapter is to show that; despite claims around 1900, that, because of the Boxer Uprising; China had forfeited the right to be called a civilisation, there was a time when it was held to possess many of the hallmarks of a civilization:- namely industrial and scientific achievements put to the benefit of the country's smooth running. There was also a time when the West viewed China more positively than at the high point of Western imperialism, the late nineteenth century. By the end of the nineteenth century,

China was in an severely disadvantaged state in comparison with the four major powers, with which she had to contend. This is chiefly because she had suffered a severe loss of self-respect, due to the loss of territory to Japan, Russia, France and Great Britain. In 1895, China had been soundly defeated in a war with Japan over conflicting interests in Korea. Chinese troops put down an anti-government uprising in Korea in 1894. Japanese troops stepped in, and after negotiations failed to bring about their withdrawal, China declared war at the beginning of August 1894. After the Chinese defeat, which exposed her powerlessness, according to the author Panikkar, `It was clear to all that corruption had eaten into her vitals...that her administration had become altogether inefficient.` [1]

The significance of China being defeated by Japan is that it indicates that the argument that there was a conflict between Orient and Occident alone is too simplistic. It also casts doubts on the `Yellow Peril` belief at that time that the West was going to face a united threat of Oriental power. China at this time faced competition for territory and influence within its borders between the great powers, Britain, France, Germany, Japan, Russia and the United States. Britain tried to contain France in Siam and Japan was availed upon to retreat from its territorial gains in China after the 1894-1895 war. `A Russian move away from Europe to the east may have been a pleasing prospect in London, but from a Far Eastern perspective her advance was menacing.` [2]

China had not always been a country racked by powerlessness and corruption. An overview of Chinese history from 1600 to 1885, illustrates that, as far as the `Yellow Peril` scare was concerned, this scare pushed firmly aside the earlier achievements of Chinese civilisation. This was clear because the achievements of Chinese civilisation are well documented, as in the six volumes of Joseph Needham's Science and Civilisation in China. Robert Temple, in his book `The Genius of China` (introduced by Joseph Needham), gives a comprehensive analysis of Chinese advances in civilization, since the discovery of lacquer in the 13th century B.C.

As far as metallurgy and astronomy are concerned, to cite a few examples from Temple's book:- The iron plough was invented or discovered 2,200 years before its recognition in the West. Manufacturing of steel from cast iron was invented during the 2nd century B.C. , 2000 years before its adoption by the West. The Chinese used iron and steel to make swords. The suspension bridge was invented by the Chinese during the 1st century A.D. possibly over 2,200 years before its advent in the West. ` Needham believes that [the Chinese] applied wrought-iron chains to suspension bridges by the 1$^{st}$ century A.D. Massive stone abutments were built to contain the chain ends.` [3] As far as astronomy is concerned, the Chinese were well ahead of those in the West in certain areas. For example, the Chinese recognized the significance of sun spots as solar phenomena during the fourth century B.C. , two thousand years before the West. ` Needham has counted the numbers of sunspot observations in the official histories between 28BC and 1638 AD and has found 112 instances.` [4] `The Chinese discovered the solar wind in the 6$^{th}$ century A.D., a total of one thousand four hundred years before the West. According to Temple: `It is now known that comet tails always point away from the Sun because they are so tenuous that the force of the `solar wind` pushes them away into that position. `[5] With regard to chess: ` Although most historians of chess believed that the game was invented in India, Needham has been able to establish that it originated in China. Chess took its present form as a militaristic combat game in India, but its origins were connected with astrology, magnetism and divination.` [6] Finally, at some point as far back as at least 2400 B.C. the Chinese began to measure astronomical events using the equator for observations. This was not adopted in the West until the time of Tycho Brahe, (1576-1601.)

It is important to highlight the achievements of Chinese civilisation to expose the deficiencies of the `Yellow Peril` idea, because this idea was, to a large extent, based upon a premise that the Chinese were barbarian and not civilised and therefore dangerous.

The Ming Dynasty is China's golden age of expansion and exploration and trade. The Ming Dynasty ended in 1643, to be succeeded by the Ch'ing (Qing) Dynasty: (1644-1911) `The Ming Dynasty is thought of as a glorious period in Chinese history, art, literature and scholarship flourished. ` [7] This was also the period during which the famous blue and white porcelain, which became popular in Britain was produced. The period 1662 to 1723, was the culmination of the ceramic art period in China, and there were labourers based in Canton (Guangzhou) manufacturing the ceramics for the European market. The enthusiasm for things Chinese from the end of the seventeenth century included tea, silk, enamel, glass and lacquer. Porcelain was produced in Britain, which copied the Chinese style. Great novels which were still popular in the twentieth century and translated into English, such as Water Margin and Journey to the West, were written in this period.

By 1600, the Chinese had hundreds of years of experience of "barbarians" from beyond their borders. The barbarians were thought of in this way because they were not Han Chinese. Han Chinese were Chinese peoples as distinct from national minorities such as Tibetans, Miao, and Mongols. This experience came through ventures such as the voyages of the eunuch Zheng He to as far afield as the coast of East Africa in about 1417.

The Ming dynasty(1368-1643AD) was roughly contemporary to the Renaissance and Reformation in

Europe. At its start China was still probably ahead of Europe in terms of cultural achievement, but by its close Europe was ahead in terms of science and technology. When the eunuch Zheng He led his famous fleet of giant ships around the South China Sea and Indian Ocean as far as Zanzibar in seven voyages between 1405 and 1433, he went with imperial patronage. His first voyage to South East Asia, Sri Lanka and India consisted of 28,000 men in 62 huge vessels. The scale of these vessels and voyages dwarfed the more famous voyage of Columbus to the New World some 90 years later. [8]

The Chinese failed to build upon the success of Zheng He's voyages and by 1450 the mighty ships which had sailed towards Africa were decomposing wrecks. We may take the failure of China to capitalize upon Zheng He's voyages as a symbolic sign of a greater underlying weakness which led China into a period of catastrophic decline just when the West was poised to forge ahead through the Age of Exploration into the Industrial Revolution [9]

The Chinese practice was to include those states on the borders of the Middle Kingdom, such as Korea and Burma, in a system of payment of tribute. In return for this, these states would come under Chinese influence. By sending tribute, those states acknowledged the authority of the Chinese Emperor. The first Western trade missions to China were only acceptable by the Chinese as tribute missions. In the early seventeenth century, individuals were visiting China with knowledge, not necessarily tribute, which was at that time complementary but not always superior to Chinese knowledge, an example being Jesuit knowledge of astronomy. In 1582 the Jesuit Matteo Ricci arrived in Macao, and he became established in Peking in 1600. Jesuits became established in the Imperial Court, for nearly two hundred years after this, imparting Christian teachings and Western knowledge. Ricci's diaries of his time in China proved very popular. They were translated into German, Italian, French and Spanish. Excerpts were translated into English and in the decade following 1615 the work was reprinted four times in Latin. This diary was therefore undoubtedly a major source of images received in the West about China at the time. Ricci's book described Chinese achievements in medicine, classics, astronomy and mathematics. Images of China presented to the West at this time were relatively positive.

Ricci was very impressed by China's wealth, 'Everything which the people need for their well-being and sustenance, whether it be for food or clothing or even delicacies and superfluities, is abundantly produced within the border of the kingdom.' [10] Ricci, however, noted the overwhelming power of magistrates, over the life or death of the criminal and the severity of punishment. This image of a brutal and corrupt Chinese judiciary survived into the early twentieth century. Astronomy was very important to the Chinese rulers in the seventeenth century. Jesuits had positions of responsibility in government as astronomers. If a "civilisation" can be said to be a condition of intellectual, cultural and moral refinement, then in the intellectual realm, Chinese astronomy reached its peak in the twelfth century, four hundred years ahead of Europe' [11] and a century before Marco Polo was alleged to have visited China. Not only were the Chinese ahead of the West, in astronomy at one point, but they were also more advanced in metallurgy. Zinc production began in N. India one thousand years ago, but collapsed within the last few hundred years due to Chinese imports. 'In 1739 a British company attempted to patent the Indian process with huge smelting cones, but this failed totally. There was grudging praise of Chinese zinc production in early 20th century British trade journals.' [12] This praise was grudging because according to the prevailing wisdom of the times; the West was superior in industrial technology.

China did not only have some of the hallmarks of a civilisation, from the beginning of the seventeenth century onwards, but it was superior to some other countries in certain scientific and industrial areas such as navigation, astronomy and metallurgy. The aspect of her affairs which were "civilized" were the harnessing by the state of these talents, for the improvement of the nation and smooth running of the Government. The racism of portrayals of the Chinese three hundred years later totally deleted this aspect of Chinese culture from their accounts. This racism forgot that in the late seventeenth century, China had opened up communications with the West. In 1686 a Chinese man called Shen Fu Tsong, (Shen Fu-zong or Michael Alphonsus,c.1658-1691) a Jesuit convert from Nanking, became established at the court of James II and became the first person to catalogue the Chinese collection at the Bodlean Library in Oxford.

Shen apparently met the Orientalist and Bodley's librarian Thomas Hyde in London, subsequently writing to him from there on 25 May 1687. Shen travelled to Oxford for the summer and helped Hyde with several projects on Chinese measurement, calendrical practices, and games by producing both translations and samples of Chinese writing for copperplate engravings. [13]

He was a: Traveller and convert to Christianity, was born at Nanking (Nanjing) in Kiangnan (Jiangnan) province along the southern side of the Yangtze(Yangzi) River in the (Ching) Qing empire. His father, a physician, probably converted to Catholicism in the 1670s. Following this the young Shen received a Christian baptismal name and met the Flemish Jesuit Philippe Couplet, who was based near Nanking. Shen clearly had some education in classical Chinese and could certainly read and write respectably, although it is unclear if he ever had ambitions to take the official exams. He also learned some Latin and was selected to join Couplet on a trip to Europe to promote the activities of the mission. Shen was not the first visitor to Europe from China nor was he probably the first Chinese person to visit England, as records of East India Company voyages indicate Chinese diaspora merchants living in Bantam would replace English and other sailors lost on the arduous voyage. Nevertheless, Shen had the greatest impact on both Chinese scholarship and courtly politics in Europe and particularly in England of any traveller from China during the period. [14]

Later, Chinese arrived with the East India Company which was importing Chinese commodities such as silks, ceramics and tea. (A Chinese man named John Anthony took on the role of looking after Asian sailors whilst they were in London and by 1805 he had accumulated both the influence and money, to become the first Chinese man to be naturalised as a British citizen. That required an Act of Parliament or a Bill of Naturalization. His obituary was published in *The Gentleman's Magazine* of August 1805) Referring to his death, the obituary runs:

> Aged about 39, at his country-house at Hallowall-down, Essex, Jn. Anthony, esq. for whom a Bill of Naturalization passed into a law in March last. His body was removed to his residence in Shadwell, to be attended to that church by all the Chinese in town. He was the first instance of a Chinese having been naturalized in this country, where he had accumulated a great fortune, and bore a most excellent character, having for several years past been entrusted, by the Directors of the East India Company, with the care of the Chinese and Lascars employed in navigating their shipping to and from China. About six years ago he abjured Paganism and embraced Christianity. Before his death he gave directions where he would be buried, which was in Shadwell church, where he was baptised. He was carried to the grave in a hearse drawn by six horses, preceded by four natives of China dressed in white, being the mourning of their country, with four lighted wax-tapers in their hands. Two mourning-coaches followed, with the friends of the deceased, and above 2000 of the neighbouring poor and other persons. [15]

In 1736, the Jesuit Jean-Baptiste Du Halde published The General History of China. Although he is now considered to be the greatest author of his age on China, he never actually went there. His source was a collection of monographs and letters, etc, written by Jesuits who had visited China since 1703. This collection was called the *Lettres edifiantes et curieuses*. The General History of China was one of the key documents on China at the time, 'Du Halde was immensely positive about China. He praises virtually every aspect of its people and society, and where he offers criticism it is in a defensive tone as if he regarded himself as an advocate for China. `[16] Elsewhere, Du Halde described China as being a country of great wealth. (There was a time therefore when Western commentators were actually impressed with China, before the peak of Western imperialism about 150 years later.) This confirms the reason the Ch`ing government gave to MacCartney about 60 years later, for refusing to open up trade with Britain. This was that China already had all it needed to survive. It was this belief that led the Chinese Government official, who saw MacCartney, Ch`ien Lung, to report to George III that China had `all things in prolific abundance.` This was not just a policy statement, but an expression of the Chinese belief that to trade with the foreigner was against the reputation of China.

A severe problem, which was symptomatic of the lack of foresight in China up to the eighteenth century, and similar to the Japanese position up to the mid nineteenth century, was that China was prepared to let in Western knowledge, but not accept the consequences and responsibilities. China was not prepared to "play the diplomacy game" whilst maintaining the illusion that she was the Throne of Heaven. If China was receiving a British delegation, the sensitivities of diplomacy should have followed, but in practice did not. Thus, when the British delegation under MacCartney visited Peking on September 14th 1793, with `600 hundred packages of presents, borne by 3,000 coolies` (*The Guardian* December 10 2005.[17] `Enter the dragon.`) and a banner in Chinese declaring, `Ambassador bearing tribute from the country of England`[18] MacCartney was expected to kowtow, but refused. (In fact it became a point of controversy between Britain and China as to whether or not MacCartney *did* kowtow. MacCartney was well prepared for his visit to China. According to his note book held in the Bodlean Library, Oxford, MS Eng. misc. f.534 page five, he noted that the Chinese Emperor rose at 3am and went back to bed at 7pm.) MacCartney also observed a number of other things about Chinese culture and politics. In notes entitled `China-Women ` : he comments on footbinding (page 3) and on the same page: ` Pearls are used in Medicine in China for complaints in the stomach in external applications.` On page 4 of the notebook there is a comment that the Emperor had "one hundred concubines." Later (page 5) MacCartney astutely comments :

> 'What great right have we to complain of Chinese or other foreigners for resisting our trade when in Henry VIII`s reign foreigners were either most heavily taxed or obliged to leave the kingdom.`

China was unaware of the different values of the West and expected British delegates to act like the emissaries of an immediate neighbour. Initially Chinese leaders underestimated the lengths to which the West would go to press its economic claims in their country, and China's military might at the time of the First Opium War, (1840-1841), was no match for the British. British expansion into China was initially dictated by reasons of trade. Earlier, in 1816, there had been another unsuccessful trade mission from Britain to China, under Lord Amherst, which floundered over the refusal of Amherst to kowtow. The mood of China's rulers at that time is summarised in the following terms:

Europeans were treated as barbarians by Chinese officials, with whom direct communication was forbidden. The Chinese adopted a rigid attitude; if the Europeans did not like the conditions, or did not wish to obey Chinese laws, they could return home, because China was self-sufficient and had no need of the products of any other country. [19]

A little later, in about 1824, school children in Britain were being given the following impression of China, from *A Grammar of General Geography for the use of Schools and Young Persons*:

> China is a world within itself, the people despising all other nations, never making foreign wars, and living on their own produce and manufactures, cultivating the religion of Confu-

cius, and their own arts and sciences, and preserving the same dresses, manners, and pursuits from age to age. [20]

Relationships were not only poor between Europeans and Chinese. In Hong Kong there was bad feeling at times between Europeans, as in the case of the German civil servant E.J. Eitel who wrote *Europe in China. The history of Hong Kong from the beginning to 1882.*

He `was made a naturalised British subject by the Governor's special ordinance. The rise to place and power of this forty-year old foreigner naturally exacerbated the British officials of the Hong Kong Government, one of whom described it as `terribly galling.` [21]

China's power declined throughout the whole of the nineteenth century, just as Britain's economic and political power was rising, as exemplified by the fact that Britain was prepared to expand economically and territorially, eastwards from India towards China. Eventually, the British tried a more forceful policy on the implementation of trade with China, particularly that of opium. This was in rivalry with other European powers. By the early nineteenth century, Britain had become the major land power in South Asia. Soon, British attention became focused on obtaining footholds on the Chinese coast for protection for maritime trading vessels. After the defeat of Napoleon, Britain gained unprecedented moral, political and economic predominance in relation to other European powers . Between 1815 and 1848, Britain and Russia were the major powers in the East. The Industrial Revolution of the eighteenth century gave Britain an advantage which, allied with her strong maritime trade, meant that it was only a matter of time before there was a clash between mercantilist, laissez faire British trade and very conservative Chinese officials. In 1833 the monopoly of the East India Company, then almost dead as a power, was cancelled by Parliament. As a result of this, trade in the South China Sea became a much freer affair:

The triangular pattern of trade between Britain, India and China had developed and become well established during the first half of the nineteenth century. British purchases of tea, silk and other exports from China were balanced by the export to China by India of Indian cotton and opium; the triangle was completed by the export by Britain to India of goods and services. [22]

In the ninth century A.D. Arabs took opium to China and during the sixteenth century the Portuguese did likewise. In 1838, the import of opium into China reached a peak of forty thousand chests. This trade led to severe social and economic problems in China. The Chinese bureaucracy were not passive in their acceptance of the import of opium, but they were unable to do anything about it, because of the much greater military power of the West. Just over thirty years later a China based missionary was to write: `Opium smoking is rampant in all parts, and is eating out the vitals of the nation.` [23] Opium smoking in southern China was seen by Chinese government officials as leading to social decay and as a threat to social control. Fortunately we in the West have an insight into the Chinese attitude towards "opium eating" within its boarders and the British attempts to export opium to China. The activity of the Chinese bureaucracy can be shown in the measures of Imperial Commissioner Lin Tse-hsu in Canton. On June 3rd 1839 he forced British merchants in Canton to hand over about 20,000 chests of opium in order to try and suppress the opium trade. These he destroyed. This was the pretext for the British to go to war against China, during which the island of Hong Kong was seized permanently. Reports by the Chinese and the British concerning the fortunes of their own particular military forces in the war were widely divergent:

On June 12th [1841] [Lin] hears that on May 21st there was a great victory at Canton. Seven foreign ships were burnt or otherwise destroyed, and seven rebel foreigners were captured alive. Innumerable casualties were inflicted. On June 15th he hears that there has been another engagement and a certain amount of damage inflicted on the enemy. On June 17th he gets a letter from I-liang, the Governor of Kwangtung, dated May 31st, saying that after May 22nd the rebel foreigners had again become violent, but had then once more pleaded for peace. `I do not know yet what sort of report he [ i.e. Ch`I Kung [a]] is sending about this.

The English accounts tell us only that on May 21st and during the ensuing days the last remaining defences of Canton were destroyed, and that on May 27th the Chinese agreed to pay six million dollars as a bribe to the English to withdraw. Only trifling damage to ships is mentioned and there is, I think, no admission of any casualties. The English account is certainly more credible than that of the Chinese; for if the Chinese had scored a great victory, it is hard to see why they had to bribe off the attackers. [24]

In the Treaty of Nanking on August 29th 1842 the Chinese Government had to pay twenty one thousand dollars compensation for the opium destroyed and open up four additional ports to British subjects and consuls. These were Amoy, Foochow, Shanghai and Ningpo. By 1912, there were well over fifty ports open to foreigners in China. Commissioner Lin made a lot of bluster about destroying the British fleet stationed off Hong Kong by Kowloon Point during June 1839 but this never happened. Several months later Lin boasted:

> Since the English established their blockade of our ports other foreigners have been complaining bitterly, and are about to send warships to bring the English to their senses. But the fact that they are in a hopeless position makes them try to cover up their weakness by adopting an even more arrogant and bullying attitude than before. However, when all their villainous devices have failed they will have nothing for it but to bow their heads and submit [25]

The Chinese Emperor saw through Lin`s constant attempts to gloss over Chinese military losses in their attempt to hinder British ships` attempts to export opium and establish safe defensive positions in the vicinity of Hong Kong.

During the war the Emperor had consistently laid the blame for everything that went wrong upon other people…….he was quite wrong in thinking that China`s defeat was due to the inexperience of her military leaders. Superiority of fire-power and command of the sea and of the major waterways were what made the English invincible. No generalship, however talented or experienced, could have made the course of events go differently. But the Manchus were a conquering race and were reluctant to accept the fact that the weapons with which they had conquered China two hundred years ago were now out of date. [26]

About seventy years later Chinese opium taking, allegedly in Britain, Hong Kong and China, became a part of the racial stereotyping of Chinese. This will be examined further in the chapter on the `Yellow Peril.` The double standards of the British are exposed, when it is remembered that it was this nation which accepted opium trade activities for almost a century after the 1830s, and yet condemned Chinese opium consumption in literature; such as children's magazines in the early twentieths century. (`A widespread persecution of Christians broke out in 1839 after Britain attacked China.` [27] In the mid Nineteenth century to most Chinese becoming a Christian was an act of betrayal, as the general perception was that Christianity was a tool of Western imperialism. It was said , `one more Christian, one less Chinese.` [28])

The determination of the British to back up the export of opium to China with military force was hardly met with unequivocal support by influential voices in Britain. The *Manchester Guardian* at the time

---

[a] Ch` I Kung was the President of the Board of Punishments.

stated that, The opium question is, however, an exceedingly difficult question to deal with; and we do not at present foresee any speedy or satisfactory solution to it.` [29] In fact, when the sale of opium to China was banned in 1903,` ..its sale still provided 8 per cent of the Indian government's revenue.` [30] In 1856, the Second Opium War took place between Britain and China. The circumstances surrounding the outbreak of this war, related to a ship called the Arrow. In October 1856, the Arrow, with a British flag, entered the Pearl River delta near Canton. The vessel was boarded by a Chinese patrol looking for pirates, during which time the British flag was lowered and some Chinese sailors arrested. When the Chinese refused to return the arrested sailors, this led to the occupation of Canton by a thousand British soldiers. The final outcome was the Treaty of Tientsin of June 26th 1858. This treaty, was one of what became known as the "unequal treaties", which was a phrase the Chinese Communist Party came to use from time to time, during the negotiations over the handing back of Hong Kong. The significance of this phrase "unequal treaties" is threefold. Firstly it shows the dual nature of the British Imperial venture. There were unequal or unbalanced values. On the one hand, imperialism was seen by its pioneers as partially a philanthropic venture, of benefit to the natives of the country being occupied. On the other hand, if these natives exhibited signs of resistance to British intrusion or self-assertiveness, this was met with military intervention, as in China between the 1830s and 1920s and in India during the Mutiny. These two incidents in British Imperial history cannot be realistically compared in any other way, except as in cases of British Imperial might being challenged by what could very loosely be described as national liberation movements. Secondly, unusually for phrases that have been picked up and popularised by the late Twentieth century news media, the phrase "unequal treaty" is near the reality of what did occur between China and the West. For example, in 1858, treaties were made between Britain, France, Russia and the United States, ending the Arrow or Second Opium War. The Chinese gained nothing and lost further ground to the "great powers." The West was allowed the right to have ministers in Peking; ten new ports were opened to the West, and freer travel into the interior was granted to missionaries and traders.

Between 1860 and 1895, as missionaries of various denominations penetrated into the interior to carry out their work of conversion, there was a steady growth in anti-foreign feeling which manifested itself in sporadic outbursts of violence on the part of the populace. [31]

Even before this missionary activity created anti-foreigner feeling in parts of China:

The result (of French military action near south-west China in 1847) was a blood bath. When an angry mob drove one particular (French) missionary out of a city they cried after him: " You burned our palace, you killed our emperor, you sell poison to our people, and now you come professing to teach us virtue! "[32]

By about 1830 missionaries entered:

> ".A period of translation and of the key backing to the idea of translation, the first composition of a good Chinese English dictionary in which the languages were shared and pulled together by, actually, missionary scholars at the same time as they compiled their dictionary to translate the whole of the Bible into Chinese. And this feat was finished with the first draft version around about 1830.[33]

The Times of December 26th 1869 commented, " China was an oyster, to be opened"[4] *The Illustrated London News* put forward the following opinion less than six months later:

> What a prospect is hereby opened up to us! What space for the expansion of trade! What an endless variety of new resources does it bring within reach! What an expanse for the

exertion of scientific, literary, philanthropic and religious enterprise!....It is as though Western energy had recovered for itself a third part of the globe, for nearly two centuries as good as lost to it. [35]

The third significant feature is that these treaties still had the power to wound the national pride of the Chinese, for such a long time after their imposition. The ability of foreign intervention in China to influence nationalistic feelings and racial attitudes was noticed by Han Suyin, a biographer of Mao. According to her, although she gives no source for the quote; Mao in the 1930s remembered a poem, read by a pro-Japanese teacher commemorating the defeat of Russia by Japan in the Russo-Japanese War of 1904-5. Mao said or wrote, `I knew and felt the beauty of Japan, and felt something of her power and might....I did not think there was also a barbarous Japan...` [36]

China's national pride was not always as wounded, as Chinese politicians suggested over the Hong Kong issue in the 1980s and 1990s. If this were so then Western scholars would have been shunned. Yet Mao`s testimony as published in his Selected Works was that from China's defeat in the Opium War of 1840-41 to 1917, Chinese intellectuals (including himself), read from Western thinkers such as Darwin and Rousseau but they became disillusioned because of Western imperialism. Before 1911, in the 1870s and 1880s Chinese classics such as Confucius and similar works had been translated from Chinese into English by Chinese scholars and published by British publishing houses. After 1911 young Chinese intellectuals became interested in Marx. This interest in Marx coincided with the Bolshevik Revolution in Russia, and seems to have marked a decisive break with the West, in the attitude of a fairly significant number of young Chinese intellectuals between the years 1917 and 1921. It was during this time that the Chinese Communist Party was in its formative years. Shanghai was a particular gravitational point for those Chinese intellectuals, who had experienced Western imperialism first hand. The British media, particularly the Shanghai-based *North China Herald*, and taking its lead, Hong Kong's *South China Morning Post,* characterised the leftist Chinese students as being mindless stooges of the Russian Bolshevik government.

Between 1841 and 1917, the Chinese were still putting forwards an unrealistic point of view, with regards to the dependency of foreigners on Chinese exports. The following quotation is from the late 1890s, with regards to the situation in China about fifty years before, `people argue that it was the granting of trade that brought on our troubles. But this is absurd; for China can do without foreigners, whilst foreigners are dependent on us for tea and rhubarb, and therefore are at our mercy.` [37] `The belief that foreigners, and particularly the English, would die of constipation if deprived of rhubarb was widely held at this time in China. `It had its origin....in the practice, so widely spread in early nineteenth-century Europe, of a grand purge every spring, rhubarb-root being often an ingredient in the purgatives used.` [38] This was unrealistic and somewhat comic because it disregarded, perhaps through ignorance, that Britain and other "great powers" could survive without these products!

The culmination of the Second Opium War was the looting of Peking by British troops in 1860. *The Pall Mall* magazine of February 1895 described the looting by the French thus:

> `Their camp is a wonderful spectacle of loot; the grass is everywhere strewn with silks, satins, and rich embroideries, clocks, articles of pure gold and silver, jade ornaments, porcelains, and enamels in marvellous profusion. T'is a scene that will remind you of the great prize auctions at Delhi.` [39]

There was a severe breakdown in relations between Chinese and British in Hong Kong in early 1857, which led to physical attacks on Westerners and arson attacks on Western property. There was an incident on January 15th 1857 in which hundreds of the European community were poisoned by arsenic in the bread from the Esing bakery, including the family of Sir John Bowring, the Governor. The Governor did not carry out the drastic measures advocated by the local justices of the peace who, `...entreated the Governor to proclaim forthwith martial law and to deport every Chinaman whose loyalty could not be vouched for.` [40]

The beliefs of two Hong Kong Governors, John Bowring (1854-1859), and Sir John Pope-Hennessy (1877-1882), are revealing in how they had an effect on events in Hong Kong. Bowring was a disciple of Jeremy Bentham and a firm believer in free trade. In March 1849, whilst Consul at Canton, Bowring wrote to a relative, `There is a shocking want of truthfulness among the Chinese....So in all the courts there is an infinite difficulty in getting at facts they have no conscience, no code to which you can appeal.` [41] Bowring also had an imprudent streak. The combination of these two attributes contributed towards the Second Opium or Arrow War; which added Kowloon to Hong Kong in the Treaty of Tientsin. The Second Opium War was in effect a continuation of the First. The irony was that he was a member of the Peace Society. His experiences in Hong Kong indicated that his policies towards China, exposed a certain vulnerability within this impatient mercantilist and that he displayed an ignorance of the advantages of subtle diplomacy:

In England he could advance his ideas with articles in the *Westminster Review* and speeches in the House of Commons. On the continent, even in Egypt, there were rulers willing to be lectured and advised. But in China the choice lay between smothering his passion for progress and sending in the gunboats. [42] An issue of The London Journal in either 1856 or 1857 described Bowring as an, `advocate of every measure calculated to promote the principle of liberty.` [43]

Sir John Pope-Hennessy was an equally complex and controversial person. He was an Irish Catholic Liberal Home Ruler who advocated rights for those who found themselves subjects of British rule in Hong Kong and other colonies such as Barbados and Mauritius. His liberal policies clashed with British opinion in the local media, such as when the China Mail in August 1877, criticised his allegedly liberal policies on Chinese criminals, releasing some early. [44] It did not help relations with colonists that he was an Irish Catholic liberal, arriving in a conservative English and Protestant-dominated community. Indeed, in a rather negative review of Pope-Hennessy`s Governorship, a history of British possessions in Asia published almost thirty years after his time in Hong Kong, stated quite positively: `He was a man of peculiar temperament and endowed with more than a common share of the pugnacity which is traditionally attributed to his race.` [45]

The context of Pope-Hennessy`s nationality was that he was Governor of Hong Kong at a time, when there were growing aspirations for a self governing Ireland, `Because of this, suspicions and prejudices about the race, religion, and culture of the Irish in imperial service, were formed and reinforced.` [46]His apparent tactlessness and attempts to improve the lot of local Chinese did not help matters. In these moves to diminish racial inequality and segregation, he preferred to consult the Chinese community. He appointed the first Chinese person to the Legislative Council, Ng Choy, a barrister. The gap between Hennessy and the Colonial Office in their attitudes towards the Chinese can be seen in the increase in the representation of Chinese among the top eighteen ratepayers. In 1876 there were more non-Chinese than Chinese ratepayers. By 1881, out of the eighteen top rate payers only one was non-Chinese. Hennessy interpreted this as a sign of economic progress among the Chinese to be welcomed, whereas officials in London feared it was an attempt by Chinese to buy back Hong Kong for China. Another area of controversy between the Governor, wealthy Chinese, the Hong Kong British media and the Colonial Office was Hennessy`s patronage of the Tung Wah. This was a quasi-official institution with some influence over the Chinese population. But it was seen by colonists as having too much influence. The period of Hennessy`s office was one of stalemate with the British colonist population. It is possible that the nationalist riots that broke out in Hong Kong in 1884 were partly a result of hopes raised then unfulfilled after Pope Hennessy, was replaced as Governor by W.H Marsh then Sir George Bowen.

Edward Said has erroneously suggested that there was a homogeneous Western approach to the Orient in the era of Imperialism. In fact, the case of Japan shows that this was far from true. From about 1900 to 1921, Britain and Japan enjoyed a special relationship in the face of Russian expansion in Manchuria and Korea and German expansion in China. There was an interest in Britain in things Japanese, such as Japanese samurai and Japanese opera. Baden Powell compared Britain and Japan as two plucky island nations. From 1895 onwards, Japan ordered several battleships, to be built in British naval yards, and in 1900 Japan helped put down the Boxer Uprising at Britain's request. There was pro-British feeling in Japan around this time for three reasons. These were, British neutrality in the Sino-Japanese war of 1894, Britain not joining the Triple Intervention of Russia, France and Germany which forced Japan to give up the Liaotung Peninsula after the victory of Japan in the 1894 war and British protests against Russian aggression in Manchuria. The first Anglo-Japanese Agreement was signed on January 30th 1902 and the Second on August 12th 1905. The Second Agreement respected Japanese rights in Korea, and in turn the Japanese respected Britain's special interests in India. After the 1905 Agreement; Britain had more of a chance of concentrating her navy in European waters, to meet the challenge of the expanding German navy. During World War One, British troops and her navy fought under Japanese command, to take the German-owned town of Tsingtao into Japanese possession. Furthermore, the Japanese navy patrolled the Pacific north of the equator to protect shipping from the German navy whilst the British patrolled south of the equator. In 1921 the Duke of Windsor, the future King Edward VIII, visited Japan for a four-week stay and, in the same year, the Crown Prince of Japan visited Britain. `He told the King (George V) that the Japanese navy was copied from the British, the army from the Germans and the press from the Americans.` [47] On December 13th 1921 the Anglo-Japanese Alliance was replaced by a four-power treaty between the United States, United Kingdom, Japan and France to protect each others` rights in the Pacific. This new style treaty resulted in Anglo-Japanese alienation.

Throughout the late nineteenth century, mainland Chinese frustration at foreign intrusion increased. It was to spill over into the Boxer Uprising, 1900. This was an attempt by the conservative group around the Empress Dowager to restore some dignity to a China being encroached upon by foreign powers. It became a judgement upon the last remains of Chinese isolationism, by the intervention of the Western expeditionary force to relieve the legation quarters. The story of China in the last decade of the nineteenth century is one of continuing decline and exploitation, at the hands of the West and Japan.

Images of the Boxer Rebellion

CHAPTER THREE
The Nemesis of China's Isolation: The Boxer Uprising

The 'Yellow Peril' scare must be said to be wildly unrealistic, if we take it in its literal and crudest form, a threat that the Chinese and Japanese would unite and take over the West, but in the Boxer Uprising Western and Japanese interests in China were severely threatened in a literally perilous situation. The Boxers were a semi-secret society, also known as the I Ho T'uan, or The Righteous and Harmonious Fists.

'The Boxers believed they had magical powers and that the bullets could not harm them. The society wanted to overthrow the Qing Dynasty and expel all foreigners and foreign influences. '[1]

Their siege of the embassy quarter of the major Western powers, including Britain lasted from June 20th to August 14th 1900. June 21st represented a crucial date in the entire uprising. This was the date that the Ch'ing (Qing) Dynasty joined forces with the Boxers. As a result of this siege it was written at the time, in reaction to the Boxer Uprising,' The Chinese, with all their apparent civilization, and with all their high tradition of the past, have proved themselves as barbaric at heart as any tribe of South Sea Islanders.' [2] So not only lives were lost as a result of the Uprising, but in some quarters, China's reputation as a civilised power. (Near the time of the Boxers there was debate in this same journal as to the positions of Russia and Japan, with regards to China, 'Russia and Japan are the only two Powers which can Occidentalise China ,and of the two, for the reasons already given, Japan is in the best position to do the work. [3] "The reasons already given " were that Russia was corrupt and therefore unsuitable at civilising

China. The same journal stated, 'The Japanese thoroughly understood that other yellow race across the water' [4]) Britain and Japan shared similar interests about this time. Japan played a key role in the lifting of the siege of the Western legations in Peking. Indeed this was one of Japan's first contributions to geo-political events in the Far East in conjunction with the major Western Powers.

It can be instructive to look at historical events through the eyes of contemporary observers, setting their comments in the light of the wider course of events. The following quotations are from a missionary whose name was illegible in the microfiche archives of the Methodist Missionary Society at the School of Oriental and African Studies in London. The missionary was based in Hong Kong, far away from where the drama was occurring that summer:

July 24th 1900. We are sure the Chinese are telling awful lies when they say that the legations are safe on this day and that. Nobody out here believes them and it really angers us that the people of the West should be unable to learn from experience what these people are.

On the looting that took place during the campaign to relieve the legations and other military excesses of the Western expeditionary force:

July 31st 1900. It is no use blaming the soldiers: the provocation they have received will almost justify any steps to which they go. We live in Old Testament days out here now.

The phrase "an eye for an eye a tooth for a tooth" springs to mind on reading this opinion of the missionary's. Whatever the diplomatic niceties of the time, he clearly believed that a policy of punitive measures was justifiable under the circumstances:

September 12th 1900. We want to see a joint Government of progressive Chinese and Europeans....such a government would give glorious opportunities to the Christian preacher.

According to documents held at the National Archives, CO129/299 p.474, a dispatch titled 'Disturbances in China (14/6/1900) and p.519 (16/6/1900) 774 troops were being sent to Taku in north China by way of Hong Kong. They were expected to arrive in Taku on 21/6/1900. On p.554 of CO 129/299 it is reported that Christians living in Canton were departing for Kowloon.) Christians were slaughtered in their thousands by the Boxers. The Boxer Uprising provoked anxiety rather than panic in Hong Kong. Governor Blake sent a telegram to Chamberlain, Secretary of State for the Colonies, in Britain (CO 129-300 p..7) stating, 'protection of Treaty ports on Yangtze [river] may probably prevent spread of the Boxer movement to the Southern provinces. Blake also said in the same telegram that it was 'important Hong Kong garrison be kept at full strength....'

However:

> The assumption that the central and southern provinces of China remained in ignorance of the situation in the north cannot be maintained: at an early stage of the crisis Boxer placards imitating those posted in Peking had appeared throughout the countryside. The Imperial decree of 25th of June [1900] giving the Chinese version of events at Taku had been published in the Canton newspapers by the 29th [of June 1900] [5]

Sentiments of trusting in British strength and initiative, come close to those of the Chinese reformer, Sun Yat Sen:- who said, in a speech in 1923 to students at the Hong Kong University, that the British had done more in just under one hundred years of rule in mainly Chinese Hong Kong, than the Chinese alone had done in several centuries of rule in China, because of the lack of corruption under the British.

Sun Yat Sen may have been implying here that some sort of Government along Western lines was what worked best for China and Hong Kong. It is striking that here we have a senior Chinese politician who is not speaking out about foreigners as "foreign devils", which was the traditional Nineteenth century way of thinking among certain Chinese politicians, but speaking respectfully of the British. Referring to the situation just before the 1894-1895 China-Japan war; the American magazine Atlantic Monthly for August 1899 was more pessimistic, this time looking at Westerners opinions:

How long the nations of the West might have indulged in pleasant dreams of a self-instructed Chinese monarchy holding out both hands for the world's commerce and civilization, varied by that strange recurrent nightmare known as "the `Yellow Peril" it is difficult to say. But the internal ferment and consequent expansion of Japan hastened the awakening. [6]

The triple intervention (over the Sino-Japanese War of 1895) revealed Great Britain's isolation in the east, and the activities of the powers threatened to undermine the British position in China. [7]

Also, `The Yellow Peril` bogey was transferred to Japan` [8] on that nation's defeat of China in the war over Korea. Japan never provided the kinds of racial problems in Britain that Chinese labour was perceived to. There were anti-Japanese riots in San Francisco around 1907 though over Japanese immigration. The views of the above mentioned missionary are quite hardline, but they do not specifically cite China as a `Yellow Peril.`

An outline of the causes and course of the Boxer Uprising is as follows: In 1899 a conservative group of politicians, headed by the Empress Dowager, decided to re-invigorate the local militia in the provinces of Shansi and Shantung; these militia were infiltrated by the Boxers who were virulently anti-Christian. By the autumn of 1899, Chinese Christians were being persecuted by the Boxers, and on New Year's Eve, an English missionary was murdered. The Boxers were anti-foreign as well as anti-Christian. In June 1900, after the expeditionary force of Germans, British, Americans and Japanese, and smaller divisions from other European countries seized the Taku forts, to clear the approach to Peking and Tientsin, the siege of the legations and the Catholic cathedral began. Many Chinese and Western Christians were killed by the Boxers in Hopeh, Shansi and Manchuria.

The first European casualty of the Boxer Uprising was Reverend S.M. Brookes, a young British clergyman of the Society for the Propagation of the Gospel. He was killed in the Fei-ch`eng district of Shantung on December 30[th] 1899. `At the beginning of June, (1900) Robinson and Norman, two missionaries of the Church of England mission at Yung-ching, were murdered.` [9] The Boxers elsewhere in China were suppressed by the authorities. By July 25th information was received by Sir Henry Blake, Governor of Hong Kong from Scott, Consul at Canton, that ministers and foreigners in Canton were safe. However anti foreign feeling was reported from just across the border in China in Shamchun with pro Boxer placards being posted up. On August 14th, the legation quarters were relieved, by the expeditionary force after those under siege had survived with homemade weapons at their disposal. *The Times* of London had been erroneously publishing obituaries of significant individuals in Peking. The total number of British casualties in defence of the legations was, in military terms, 3 killed and 22 wounded and 2 civilians killed and several wounded. Fatalities in China as a whole amongst foreigners were 240 British dead, 112 American and Swedish, 79 French, 26 Belgian and Dutch, 11 Italians, 10 German, 1 Swiss, 1. The capital was looted by the foreign troops and the Imperial Court fled to Sian. In October 1900 the French sent 1,000 troops from Haiphong to Canton. The state of South Australia (this was just before Federation) sent a ship of light draught but heavy armament the " Protector" to Chinese waters to support the allied effort against the latter country:

A smooth, pleasant, but uneventful passage to Brisbane ended the China expedition. In its main purpose

it had been disappointing. There had been no active work, especially of the kind up the great rivers where the " Protectors" heavy armament on such light draught would have been markedly useful.... [10]
By September 1901, after disagreements among the victors, a protocol was signed punishing China and imposing a treaty which among other things imposed an indemnity of four hundred and fifty million taels, to be secured by revenue from the maritime customs, which were under British control. [(1)]

At this time certain residents of the colonies and concessions in China believed that they had a special insight into what was going on inside China thanks to their geopolitical position. The cartoon below [(2)] is illustrative of this. The cartoonist is following up some of the complaints in Shanghai that the allied expeditionary force treated the Empress Dowager too kindly after their ending of the Boxers siege of the legations. The Empress was allowed to escape to Sian unpunished. Figure 1 below shows a cartoon of the Empress Dowager.

A view sympathetic to the Chinese, is to be found in *The Collected Letters of George Gissing* (the English novelist, 1857-1903.) Writing to the naturalist W.H.Hudson on July 8 1900 he states, 'Massacres apart, I greatly sympathise with the Chinese. They have never wanted us; have always done their best to exclude us; & what earthly right had we to force ourselves into their country?' [10] The Boxer Uprising is described as the nemesis of Chinese isolation because it brought its own judgement upon a China, seeking desperately to cling on to the past by throwing out "the foreigner." This was not to happen until the advent of Mao tse-tung (Mao Zedong) and the Communists forty-nine years later. Up to the 1950s onwards in China, the Boxers were looked down on as being superstitious, but from this time onwards they were presented in a more favourable, nationalistic light [(3)]. The literature of the time, if studied through the eyes of modern day theorists, can though give an insight into our imperialist past which contributed to the Uprising in the first place. One such theorist is Edward Said.

(1). A fuller account of the Boxer Uprising can be found in V.Purcell *The Boxer Uprising A Background Study* (Cambridge: Cambridge University Press, 1963)
(2) Cartoon on following page, *The Rattle* November 1900
(3) This information and other Boxer related items in this chapter from: "In Our Time" BBC Radio 4. March 19th 2009.

HER IMPERIAL MAJESTY T'SÏ HSI, DOWAGER EMPRESS OF CHINA.

As she appears in the European and American illustrated papers.   As she really is.

S. C. C. v. Country Club.

1st Day—

Biron and White
Had a bit of a fight
    In disposing of Byrne and Maclaren;
But Fate was not partial
To Drummond and Marshall
    Whose efforts at winning were barren.

    At the close of day thus matters stood—
    The Country Club, one game to the good.

2nd Day—

White and Biron
Proceeded to fire on
    The innocent Bovet and Moule,
Till they forced them to beat
What was called a retreat
    But was really a rout—on the whole.

Maclaren and Byrne
Stood up in their turn
    With Marshall and Drummond to meet 'em,
Who captured a "set"
And were happy, you bet,
    Nor cared though the Cricketers beat 'em.

A win for the Country Club, who score
Five sets against the enemy's four;
But, in games, it is only fair to state,
Fifty in all against thirty-eight.

Compare these cartoons with the photograph of the Empress Dowager on the facing page

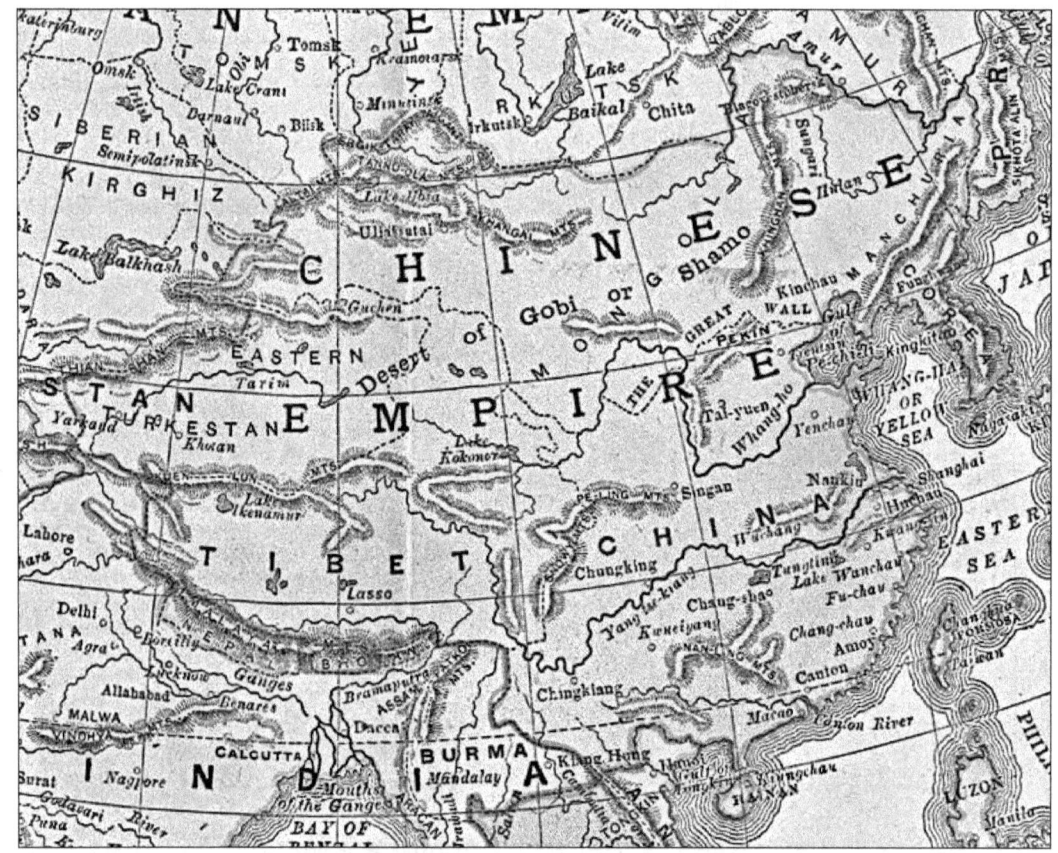

Territory of Qing China in 1892

CHAPTER FOUR
Orientalist Theories and British Imperialism in China

Edward Said's *Orientalism* and *Culture and Imperialism*, provide two viewpoints of the way the Orient has been examined. Said believed that the policy interests of Western imperialist politicians in their Eastern colonies was portrayed in a specific way. This way helped to reinforce Western dominance and created an image of the Orient as alien, whilst at the same time disempowering the colonized. It is an over-arching theory that gives little room for nuance. The Orient became a key focus of British and French imperialist power in the nineteenth century. It is not as if the Orient had no identity of its own, but it was portrayed in such a way by Western authors and politicians, in order to justify the denial to native peoples of a voice in their own affairs. The inevitable result of this, Said believed, was to polarise the difference between Orient and Occident, ruler and subject into two opposing and unequal camps, thus creating hostility. Said was influenced by Foucault who, putting his beliefs at their simplest, proposed that knowledge is used as power. However he was not in total agreement with Foucault, because Said wrote, ` ...unlike Foucault, to whose work I am greatly indebted, I do believe in the determining imprint of individual writers upon the otherwise anonymous collective body of texts constituting a discursive formation in Orientalism.` [1]

The problem with this stance, is that it inevitably draws attention to texts, known to have been of influence at a time in the past, leaving aside other less well-known texts which were more significant in popular culture. Indeed the whole tone of Orientalism, is one of concentrating on texts, suitable to the literate and elite. It seems, on the face of it, to be a classic example of Said's argument/thesis, that the relationship between East and West is one of domination, subjugation and exploitation. However, in the case of China, it is particularly unwise to argue a case based only upon a set of texts the upper- middle classes were reading and writing. This was because, in the nineteenth and early twentieth centuries, the cultural interest in China was far more socially diverse. Images of China were being conveyed to British audiences in Hong Kong and China, in the forms of photographs, theatre, `Chinoiserie`, i.e porcelain and other artefacts, propaganda films depicting staged Boxer atrocities in 1900, children's comics, satirical pieces and poems in *Punch*, Hong Kong British newspapers, etc. (For an example of `Chinoiserie` see the photograph on the following page of a statue [4] of a seated Chinese man.) There were sinologists studying China academically, such as Backhouse, J.O.P. Bland, Sir James Lockhart and Sir Reginald Johnston. These come from a long line of academics, who thought that study of China could contribute to academic understanding.

On one level, the creation of Hong Kong can be cited in a simplistic fashion as an example of Victorian gunboat diplomacy, as in the naval victory of the British in the First and Second Opium War. The advocate of Said`s approach, could argue that texts like Williams, although published after the War, were acceptable, because they existed in a climate in which Orientalism fostered a belief in ignorant, superstitious Chinese in need of civilizing British Christian Government in Hong Kong. The historical facts on the ground in Hong Kong do not support this argument fully. The prosperity and stability of Hong Kong in its early years was surely, a result of many racial and ethnic groups working successfully, though not necessarily always amicably, in the same community. There was little attempt to interfere in Chinese affairs by the British, except where local ordinances were infringed. In the case of Hong Kong, this was a port which attracted criminals and rovers; both Chinese and Western. It was also a multi-racial community. Within thirty years of it becoming a British colony, there were Indians, Malays and Africans as well as the various Chinese ethnic groups in Hong Kong. Rather than Hong Kong being moulded into an outpost of Brutishness, the Chinese community remained much as it had always been for several decades after 1841.

John Mackenzie`s approach is more even-handed, as he pays attention to Orientalism and popular culture in *Orientalism. History, Theory and the Arts*, where he states quite clearly, `Perhaps the greatest limitation on Said`s analysis of Orientalism is the fact that he concentrates almost exclusively on elite texts.` [2] A children's comic or a provincial British newspaper is hardly an elite text, but in the proper context it is still a historical document. Two examples of Orientalist texts are from the period of the two Opium Wars. In 1848, Volume One of *The Middle Kingdom* was published, written by the Protestant missionary Samuel Wells Williams. It was (and remains), one of the best-known works on China. According to archives from the collection of former Hong Kong Governor, Sir Matthew Nathan (1904-1907) at Rhodes House Library, Oxford, the two volumes of this work were on Nathan`s reading list [5] in 1904. In 1925 in a survey of one hundred mainly British and Americans living near Shanghai, out of two hundred and eleven titles *The Middle Kingdom* was the fourth most popular. The author of this survey in a Shanghai-based magazine for missionaries wanted to know which books had promoted, `a sympathetic and correct understanding of this wonderful land and its still more wonderful people.` [3] Yet Williams` work was very negative about the Chinese, seeming to undermine the optimism or ignorance of this 1925 statement, just quoted. According to Williams the Chinese, `present a singular mix of virtue and vice...if there is something to commend, there is more to blame....The result is a full unchecked torrent of human depravity.` [4]

Given its influence since its publication date onwards, it could be used as a pointer to Orientalist justifications for intrusion into China, based on an argument that such a backward people needed the benefits of British civilisation. Yet its presence so high on the above-mentioned survey may not be because it reflects the condescending attitude of the West towards China from the 1840s to 1920s, but because the survey consisted of readers sympathetic to the missionary cause. The negative tone of *The Middle King-*

---

(4) A statue of a seated Chinese man,**Fig 2** From Richard Muirhead`s collection.
(5) Archives as found at Rhodes House Library, Oxford. Sir Matthew Nathan Notebooks 1904

dom may not be surprising, but it would be dangerous to use this text to bring other "anonymous" and "diffuse" texts ,(see above Said quote) into some kind of rigid orbit. This is because these anonymous or less well-known texts might contradict the elite texts authors` self-confident belief, in their own interpretation of China and the Chinese. In 1857, close to the time of high tension in Hong Kong over the Second Opium War, Household Words contained the following,`...reasonable men amongst the Chinese laugh with bitter scorn when you bring the Bible in one hand and opium in the other.`[5] There were dissenting voices willing to credit the Chinese with patriotism and the British with hypocrisy, betraying a self-doubt grand theories tend to downplay.

Another problem, therefore, with the Saidean approach, is that it overemphasises the confidence of, in this case, British politicians or missionaries. It is worth setting two quite lengthy quotations adjacent to each other to compare two accounts of the situation with regards to Western imperialism in China. The first quotation is from Mackerras who is sympathetic towards Said. The second is from The Chinese Recorder in December 1900 shortly after the Boxer Uprising.

The whole tone of nineteenth century writings on China shows that realistic attempts to take account of non-European, for example Chinese, standards grew fainter and fainter, rarer and rarer, as the century wore on and the military, economic, political and social impact of Western imperialism strengthened.

However, the speculation in The *Chinese Recorder's* article ` Are Missionaries in any way responsible for the present disturbances in China?` was as follows:

> Look at foreign trade during the Victorian era. What are the wares brought to these shores by the merchants? Does he seek only to help a poor heathen people? Alas! Poison is sold in great chests and the Westerner rejoices in seeing the poverty and suffering, ruin and degradation his hand has wrought. [7]

This relatively enlightened tone is all the more surprising, when set against the severe loss of life among foreign and Chinese Christians during the Boxer Uprising of the previous summer. The approach of Said and Mackerras suggests the streamlining of opinion about China into a conformist standard, of unsympathetic racial stereotyping. Whilst this undoubtedly did occur, it was by no means universal. The purpose of setting the two quotations next to each other, is to show that the one overarching view of China and the Chinese, the somewhat negative approach, cannot be assumed to be the "correct" approach and that there are alternative points of view as expressed in the second quotation. An equally positive view of the Chinese is put forward by Colquhoun in his China in Transformation: ,`His predominant quality, that which marks the Chinese as a race, whether at home or abroad, is, beyond doubt, his industry` [8]

It must be remembered that there was considerable cross-cultural communication between China and Britain. The young communists such as Mao tse-tung had opportunities to go on study tours of France. Mao tse-tung was reading Kropotkin, Bakhunin and Tolstoy around about 1917 and 1918. More obviously, Britain has received inspiration in garden design and art and blue patterned porcelain from China. So to speak of cultural domination by Britain over China is inaccurate. In one area however, that of a genre of childrens` literature and politics, there has been a negative strand. This strand of thinking is the `Yellow Peril.`

THE YELLOW PERIL.
(THE GERMAN VERSION.)
Drawn, in 1895, by H. Knackfuss, from a Design by His Majesty William II., German Emperor, King of Prussia.

CHAPTER FIVE

The "Yellow Peril" - the Chinese as a Threat

From being a nation to be admired by some Europeans in the 1600s, by 1900 China and the Chinese had become the `Yellow Peril.` The origin of this phrase is obscure, though it has recently been defined as, `A scare, originally raised in Germany in September 1895 by Kaiser Wilhelm II that the yellow races of China and Japan would rapidly increase in population and overrun the territories occupied by the white races with fearful consequences.` [6] The illustration overleaf, [7] from the 1890s, depicts the German fear of the `Yellow Peril.` (in German "Gelbe Gefahr.") The Archangel Michael (this was Diosy's opinion, even though this Archangel protects Israel) beckons towards the seated Buddha, representing the Peril. The nations of Europe, represented by women, including Britain, stand cautiously in the background. The British, though, by this time were beginning to regard the `Hun` peril as far more dangerous.

Advisers to American President McKinley around 1900 warned him of a `Yellow Peril` `in relation to the Philippines which the Americans colonised in 1898. Henry Adams, an adviser, was afraid of the Japanese. Other Americans were afraid of the consequences of large scale Chinese and Japanese immigration into the United States. In 1882, the U.S. Government passed the U.S. Chinese Exclusion Act, which reduced Chinese immigration from 30,000 per year to just 105. The labour leader Samuel Gompers argued " The superior whites had to exclude the inferior Asiatics, by law, or, if necessary, by force of

---

(6) See A.Room *Brewers Dictionary of Phrase and Fable* 15th ed p.1175 (London: Cassell Publishers Ltd,1995)
(7) Cartoon opposite: Frontispiece to *The New Far East* by A.Diosy. Diosy describes the figures in the cartoon as follows, from right to left: The Buddha, the Archangel Michael, ,France, Germany, Russia, Austria, Italy,Britain, Portugal (?) and Spain (?)

Wrecked Chinese laundry damaged by rioters in Cardiff, 1911

arms"[1] The "fearful consequences" (see above quotation) were much played upon, by the authors of children's comics and some journalists in the early years of this century. Simultaneously, there still existed a fascination with China the exotic. There already existed two other visions of the Chinese. Namely "John Chinaman" and the "heathen Chinee." The phrase "heathen Chinee" came from *Plain Language from Truthful James,* a poem by Bret Harte (1836-1902), a poet best known for his descriptions of pioneering life in California, which contains the lines:

> *Which I wish to remark*
> *And my language is plain*
> *That for ways that are dark*
> *And for tricks that are vain,*
> *The heathen Chinee is peculiar.*

This poem also states quite bluntly: `We are ruined by Chinese cheap labour.`[2]

This image of the Chinese was employed in the Manchester based *Sunday Chronicle,* for December 9th 1906. The last three lines of the above poem were reproduced, almost word for word in the text of part two of a piece on the alleged dangers of Chinese vice in British ports, such as Cardiff, Liverpool and London. Part one had stated,` The immigration authorities and the public have only just awakened to the fact that England is in danger of a "yellow peril " through the formation of Chinese communities at the seaports...`[3] The piece went on to say in part two, ` They [8] are not going to accept from the Flowery Land a civilisation and morality infinitely lower than their own`.[4]

In 1911 severe unrest broke out between striking Welsh sailors and Chinese people in Cardiff. Between 1906 and 1911, both in the U.S.A. and Britain anti-immigrant fears rose amongst indigenous workers. This culminated in anti Chinese unrest in California in 1877 and in Cardiff in July 1911. Anti Chinese feelings rose in Cardiff in 1911, because of the belief that Chinese workers were working for lower wages than the Welsh on vessels and because of the belief that Chinese were strike breakers. The unrest in Cardiff at this time included attacks by rioters on Chinese owned laundries.(By the early 1900s there were hundreds of Chinese laundries around Britain.[5]) Some Chinese ended up being escorted by the police. The image opposite shows the broken windows of a Chinese laundry in Cardiff at this time.

On July 11th 1911 a crew of Chinese firemen were on board a steamship called the *Foreric* in Roath Basin, Cardiff. There were rumours that the captain "was attempting to sign on the rest of his crew"[6] The Welsh strikers ("about a score of men"[7]) stormed the ship, to be confronted by the Chinese who had drawn their knives. Soon the strike leader, a trade union leader called Tupper, agreed to contact the Foreric's owners and arrange to withdraw the Chinese. A picket of the vessel was also consented to, leaving a group of about fifty strikers in the vicinity. Tupper despatched a strong picketing party, to a vessel signing on a crew at a cheaper than normal rate, but it is not known if this was a Chinese crew.

On July 12th the situation between the strikers and Chinese workers in Cardiff continued to deteriorate. The strikers attacked an office of a tug owner, who was supposed to have "transhipped a Chinese crew"[8] from Penarth Pier to the ship the Lady Jocelyn. Stones and coal were thrown at the offices and the owners of the tug then backed down, saying that no more Chinese would be employed by the company again. At Barry, Chinese crews were withdrawn. Meanwhile, in Cardiff, " the situation, indeed, was a most ugly one."[9] On July 17th there was a dispute over Chinese sailors on board the steamship *Dulwich.* Welsh workers refused to put the ship on the blocks in the dry dock at Roath Dock, until the Chinese

---

(8) The sailors and dockers of Liverpool

aboard were paid off.

By July 20th the tension between Welsh striking seamen and Chinese sailors spilled over into violence which affected the wider Chinese community. " Almost every Chinese laundry in the city [of Cardiff] was raided and looted, and in some cases set on fire." [10] There were about two hundred Chinese in Cardiff at this time, thirty of which ran laundries all over Cardiff. The rioters moved from Cornwall Road to Paget Street and smashed the windows of laundries with stones, . the police presence being too small to stop the persecution of the Chinese. From Paget St the mob then moved on to Tudor Road and Wells Street to attack more laundries. The angry crowd, bent on destroying more Chinese laundries, moved to the Cowbridge Road area of the city and destroyed the windows of Sing Lee's premises. This place was looted and set alight, but a policeman smothered the flames. Chinese individuals in various parts of Cardiff were attacked by rioters.

The *Western Mail* of July 22nd 1911 reported that four individuals were brought before a Cardiff court in connection with the anti-Chinese disturbances of July 20th. The paper also stated: " Generally speaking the rioters exercised some element of care in order to avoid damaging the property of the Chinamen's neighbours, and adjoining premises for the most part went unscathed." [11] Hardly a comfort for the Chinese one would imagine! There was a protest outside a Chinese laundry in Penarth, Wales but no damage was done to the property. On the night of Friday July 21st there were sporadic attacks on Chinese laundries in Cardiff, but nothing on the scale of the previous night. The *Cardiff Citizen* of July 22nd 1911 commented upon the "yellow launderer": " His presence here may be such as to constitute a racial peril.....; " [12] Apart from this, newspaper reporting on the anti Chinese disturbances was free of racist remarks. The *Cardiff Citizen* later in the same article, pointed out that Britain had a very small presence in China that might now feel threatened, (as during the Boxer Uprising), just as the Chinese in Cardiff were threatened in 1911.

On the night of Saturday July 22nd 1911, there was further rioting in the vicinity of the Great Western railway station, Cardiff. This rioting did not seem to be anti-Chinese in nature, rather it was generalized opportunistic violence. However at about 6pm on July 22nd the window of " Fang Lee's Chinese laundry in Commercial Road, Newport "[13] was smashed by a passer-by. The fact that July 1911 was the hottest July of the twentieth century, would not have helped ease tensions, in places like Cardiff. It is worth quoting quite extensively from *In Search of `John Chinaman`: Press Representations of the Chinese in Cardiff 1906-1911* by Joanne M. Cayford in Llafur 5(4) 1991 to gain an extra perspective on the situation with regards to the Chinese in Cardiff at the time:

> This question of Chinese representation [in Cardiff newspapers] was a more nebulous, more insidious perception of the Chinese, framed in, let us say, `tabloid` terms. It was based on rumour, suspicion, supposition, fascination, and only partly upon fact. This was the question of the Chinese lifestyle, believed to hinge on the practice of the twin `evils` of opium smoking and alleged immorality, sexual or otherwise. [14]

According to a report in the *South Wales Daily News* in 1909, (in an interview with a Bute Street chemist), referring to sales of opium, the chemist said " I fear a considerable illicit sale is being carried on.... Opium smoking amongst Chinese in Cardiff is on the increase and it is believed that the drug is obtained from London by sources which cannot be traced." [15] In 1908 the *South Wales Daily News* commented: " One of the worst features of the growth of the Chinese colony in Cardiff is the fact that marriages are made with white girls, and it is not a rare site in Bute town to see half yellow and half white babies. These babies are not always born in wedlock." By 1911 the Chinese population was in its hundreds, rather than thousands.
Cayford goes on to say, "Press attitudes towards the Chinese community in Cardiff were thus ambiva-

lent. On the one hand they were seen as diligent workers and good launderers, whose `cleanliness left nothing to be desired.` On the other, which more than countered any positive view, they were seen as living in `indescribable squalour`, [16]....." During the disturbances of July 1911, "The boarding houses became a particular target as they were often the only refuge for Chinese sailors who had been `signed off.` According to Tupper in his memoirs [9] *Seamen's Torch*:

> `But a Chinmaman told me afterwards that the yellow men used to sell sweets to the white kids from the slums - there were dirty little sweet shops connected with some of the laundries - and the sweets were smeared with some sort of dope that fetched the eaters back like flies to a honey-pot.` [17]

The *Western Mail* newspaper in Cardiff `saw [the anti Chinese riots in Cardiff] as a question of national morality , fearing retaliation against British exiles in Hong Kong.` [18] Media writing in 1911 `did very little to confound the middle-class fear of the `Yellow Peril.` [19]

The Chinese community in Liverpool, prior to 1989, centered in the Cleveland Square, Pitt St and Frederick St areas is reputed to be amongst the oldest Chinese communities in Europe and at one point was said to be the largest in Britain. `The first wave of Chinese immigrants arrived in 1866, with the establishment of the Blue Funnel Shipping Line, a branch of the Holt Ocean Steamship Company.` [20] In 1881 there were 15 Chinese in Merseyside, in 1901: 76 and 1911: 403. ` The majority of Chinese people who came to Britain before 1920 were apparently from the Guangdong Province and Hong Kong." [21] Chinese sailors began arriving in Liverpool around the mid nineteenth century and Chinese grocers and provision merchants ` didn't begin to appear in the [Liverpool] trade directories until around 1907 but they probably existed long before then.` [22] `Four thousand five hundred and ninety five seamen of Chinese origin were serving in the British merchant marine at the time of the 1911 census of seamen.` [23] Also, `British shipping companies first started employing Chinese sailors during the Napoleonic wars to replace the British sailors who had been called up to the navy.` [24]

As was the case in Chinese communities elsewhere in the United Kingdom Chinese men took British women to be their wives. This caused controversy amongst some British commentators, but to a large extent the British women made it clear that their Chinese husbands treated them better than British men. Chinese husbands were seen as more supportive and kind and were not prone to beating up their wives or drinking alcohol to excess. ` In many cases [white] women who entered into relationships with Chinese men were either partly or completely ostracised by their parents, brothers and sisters.` [25]

In June 1911 Herman Scheffauer wrote: `But it [the appearance of the Chinese community in Liverpool] is only outwardly, (sic) for beneath its calm, dingy exterior their stir the same dark passions, instincts and racial tendencies which cause this mystic yellow people to be so misunderstood, feared and hated.` [26] . The Chinese community in Liverpool, as in other British ports were inclined to gamble, because there was so little suitable entertainment for them. Scheffauer commented in `The Chinese in England (Part Two) *The London Magazine* July 1911: `London appears to be the European headquarters for the more advanced Chinese of all classes.` and:

> What then, for England, and for Europe in general, will the future hold in store when China, oldest of the old, but youngest of modern nations, takes her place as a recognized world Power? [27]

This could almost have been written in 2009! The Chinese Seamen's Welfare Centre was opened in

---

(9) E. Tupper. *Seamen's Torch* (London: Hutchinson,1938) p.50

1917 in Bedford Street, Liverpool. It provided a place for them to gather, socialize, and hopefully get their attentions away from the gambling dens. The Chinese community in Liverpool diminished in size in the 1930s, due to the depression. In later years the Chinese community established a number of organisations, such as: 1939- Chinese Language School, 1941- The Chinese Republican Progress Club, 1944- Chinese Newspaper-the Chung Hua Chow Pao (*Chinese News Weekly*). Also in 1944 the Chinese Bank was opened in Liverpool. In 1947 the Chinese Seamen's Welfare Centre was opened and in 1956 the Liverpool Chinese Gospel Mission was established. Finally in 1961, the Chinese Seamen's Club was founded.

John Chinaman was a quaint, somewhat antiquated figure, and the "heathen Chinee" added the moral element of the depraved, uncivilised Chinese person. The picture of the "heathen Chinee", is closer to the `Yellow Peril` image than the more benevolent John Chinaman, because the former image would tend to generate more fear. The "heathen Chinee" was hopelessly depraved, a mirror image of the name Chinese gave Westerners, "foreign devil" (although the Taiping changed this to "foreign brother." The Taiping Rebellion was influenced by fundamentalist Baptist missionaries visiting China from the United States in the 1830s.) So there was an attitude to China in Britain, that pulled in opposite directions. It was as if a kind of memory of the heyday of Chinoiserie, in the eighteenth and nineteenth centuries, was vying with the racial stereotyping of the beginning of the twentieth century. For a while, the negative image prevailed. A few quotes from sources in the nineteenth century illustrate however that attitudes towards China in the nineteenth century were also negative:

It is scarcely possible to look at [the Chinese] and not to laugh. Their extraordinary cracked, whining , nasal voices, the peculiar twanging, guttural sound of language, their effeminate dress, exaggerated politeness, long tails, meagre beards, fans, beads, and embroidery have at first the effect of making one believe that they belong to some different race of beings. [28]

This same author went on to write later on: `The Chinaman is a luxurious, sensual, selfish dog, who finds little gratification in society.` [29] A few years later: `....A Chinaman is, perhaps, the most naturally cruel individual in the world, yet his pusillanimity and unwarlike character is too notorious to need remark.` [30] On China, where: ` The accumulated filth, concentrated odours, and loathsome sights prohibit close inspection on the part of sensitive strangers." [31] Taking the whole spectrum of literature studied for this book, it is apparent that at the end of the nineteenth century the British could not decide if they admired or respected China, or the Chinese or regarded her as a civilisation. It could have been that this confusion arose because of the sheer quantity and diversity of images about China. An alternative explanation, and there is no one answer, is that if China was a civilization that would invite domestic criticism of the British interventionism in China. Yet even traces of civilization in China did not protect her: `Etiquette is the life of Peking, *The Times* wrote, and if conformity to it were necessary as a means of facilitating the entrance of British commerce into China`, [32] then it must be observed. An additional factor at the beginning of the twentieth century, was that the scandal over the use of Chinese labour in the Rand in South Africa led to a fear of cheap Chinese labour in Britain. Further information about this can be found in Chapter 7. After 33 months of recruiting in China for South African gold mines, between February 1904 and November 1906, 63,296 men were contracted and shipped from north and south China `and a considerably greater number were actually mobilized.` [33] Figures from other sources put the number as 63,695, see chapter 7 below.

Two quotations, indicate that the `Yellow Peril` idea did not change the other ways of categorising the Chinese; as somewhat predictably antiquated and exotic:` To most people the Chinaman is mainly a person with a pigtail....In the main he still appears the curious creature of the Canton tea and opium days...` [34] And from the same year:

> Yet perhaps not a few have failed to realise that far away, at the ends of the earth, there really exists, at the present time, a great empire the manners of whose people are in most respects so different from our own that it might well be dubbed the land of topsy turvey. [35] One such manner was footbinding, on which matter Spence comments upon a woman he had seen or heard about: 'Her forlorn figure could serve as a symbol for China as she has been seen by many Western eyes. There she stands, innocent and in pain, beautiful but disfigured,' [36]

The tone here is one of naive awe. Perhaps the real threat from China was not its military danger to the British, but the supposed sheer racial and cultural difference between the Chinese and the British. Chinese practices such as opium-taking were seen as a threat. In the Sherlock Holmes story 'The Man With the Twisted Lip' there is a powerful depiction of how the opium den was seen in the 1890s:

> Between a slop shop and a gin shop, approached by a steep flight of steps leading down to a black gap like the mouth of a cave, I found the den of which I was in search.....above the door I found the latch and made my way into a long, low room, thick and heavy with the brown opium smoke, and terraced with wooden berths, like the forecastle of an emigrant ship. [37]

In 1913 Jack London's novel about the struggles of a working class couple in early twentieth century San Francisco, *The Valley of the Moon* was published. Towards the end of the story the hero, Billy gets into a conversation with a Jew, Mr Gunston, about the differing success rates of white and Chinese farm workers in the vicinity of San Francisco. In the course of the conversation Billy says: " Don't see why a white man can't do what a Chink can," " That sounds all right," Gunston replied. " The only objection is that the white man doesn't. The Chink is busy all the time, and he keeps the ground just as busy. He has organization, system. Who ever heard of white fatrmers keeping books?" [38]

The most blatant example of China as a threat can be seen in the wildly unrealistic, yet powerful images and words of children's magazines from about 1900 to 1925, which was the period studied. The images of China are unrealistic because China never had the amount of military power she is depicted as having in the imagery of these children's magazines. These images showed the British in the Far East as militaristic and jingoistic but the Chinese as international conspirators, against British imperial interests. This statement is based on a manageable survey of several different boys magazines, from the 1900s, 1910s and 1920s and the *Girls Friend Library* of 1925. For example in the *Boy's Friend* for week ending May 16, 1925, from 'The Lion's Revenge', about a war between Chinese/Federalist forces and British/Western forces, on Chinese soil:

> All over the Chinese Empire little battles were going on ,and the yellow men were wiping out the doctors and missionaries, the teachers and the engineers , who had come from the Western countries to work among the Chinese for their good. [39]

This image is one of the Chinese as being profoundly ungrateful. Another image put forward in children's magazines both in the mid-1920s and earlier was of the Chinese being children or child-like, especially in their use of English. Accompanying this was the condescending manner of the treatment of Chinese, thus, from the *Boy's Leader* week ending June 10, 1905:

> Why, what's the matter my boy? Won't they laugh at your funny antics?" Wun Lung dried his eyes on his pigtail. "Me want go China. Me no likee London now. Missee Fred no longer stopee. Manager say no. Wun Lung weepee. Fred patted the boy's head. [40]

Professor Jonathan Spence, the British Sinologist, in the B.B.C. Reith Lecture of 2008 has stated:
> And the countries [of the West] groped towards each other in terms of language by developing a curious hybrid mixture language, which we now call Pidgin English. I don't know how many people know Pidgin English now, but it was a kind of newly coined language form in which, using Chinese grammatical sentences and a mixture of English and Portuguese and Indian and other words, a simplified trading language was developed that let the two countries communicate. And it had an extraordinary life as a language . It let people very rapidly deal in goods and tariff issues and a few basic legal issues and some problems of the exact nature of the trade items you were dealing with. It let you handle all these things with the vocabulary of only a few hundred words. I'm not saying we should add this to our curriculum in our overburdened schools, but still it is a fascinating linguistic structure. [41]

As early as 1805, the *Edinburgh Review* reported on the Chinese language:

> There is no instance we believe on the face of the earth of a language so imperfect and artificial...Of the Chinese what more is needed to know but the singular imperfection of their language, their cowardice, uncleanliness and inhumanity. [42]

An example of the kind of unrealistic militaristic imagery from 1911, can be seen in the reproduction on of the front cover of *The Boys' Best Story Paper*, November 23rd 1911 (see opposite). This represents quite a common theme. A handful (at the most) of British or Australian scouts beat back huge armies of Chinese, threatening vital Imperial interests, in this case Australia. As can be seen from the illustration on page 50, from *The Bulletin* in 1881, who took it from an unnamed Queensland newspaper, the Chinese were considered a menace before this opinion developed in Europe. One may speculate as to the circumstances relating to its production and why this is relevant to the `Yellow Peril.` From the point of view of the time and effort put into its creation, it indicates that the magazine's editorial board took the `Yellow Peril` seriously and they expected the readers to do so too. In that case, the `Yellow Peril` idea can be seen as much more of a popular bogey and icon of strangeness, than would be suggested by the very limited publicity this expression receives today.

There is no predictable pattern within the realm of children's comics. From 1888 to 1893, there was a boys` paper called *Ching Ching`s Own*, edited by Edwin Harcourt Burrage. This was before the period when the `Yellow Peril` scare was at its height. Yet Ching Ching was a positive portrayal of a Chinese, a hero, a `wiry, crafty amiable Chinese sailor.` [43] He was revived in 1904 in the Boys' Realm. There is also a positive portrayal of the Chinese of Millwall, London, in a children's story called "Over the Water to China" by E. Nesbit, first published in 1904 in the *New Treasure Seekers* collection. In the *Girls Friend Library*, the image of the Chinese is not so overtly racist. One story studied, is more concerned with inter-personal relationships and romance between a character named Mona and an old boyfriend, Jim, on board a ship from Hong Kong to Sumatra, than attitudes towards the Chinese. This is in the issue of May 1st 1925, the "Love Stories of The Sea" edition. The Empire was very much a male affair and this is reflected in the children's literature of the time.

Although it may be very hard now to see how the China of the early twentieth century could realistically be a threat to Australia and New Zealand, this threat was taken seriously at the highest level, in that part of the world in 1908. In the late nineteenth and early twentieth centuries the New Zealand prime minister Richard Seddon pursued a `Yellow Peril` anti Chinese immigration policy: ` Measures designed to curb Chinese immigration included a substantial poll tax following imperial Japan's invasion and occupation of China, which was abolished in 1944 and for which the New Zealand government has since issued a formal apology.` [44] According to the Hong Kong *South China Morning Post* for August 27th

THE BEST STORY AND ARTICLE PAPER

THE BOYS' BEST STORY PAPER 1d.

No. 8.—Vol. I. [Registered at the G. P. O. for transmission by Canadian Magazine Post.] EVERY THURSDAY.—ONE PENNY. November 23, 1911.

"BE PREPARED"

A TALE OF WORLD-WIDE SCOUT ADVENTURE.

By E. LE BRETON MARTIN.

Author of "The Boys of the Otter Patrol."

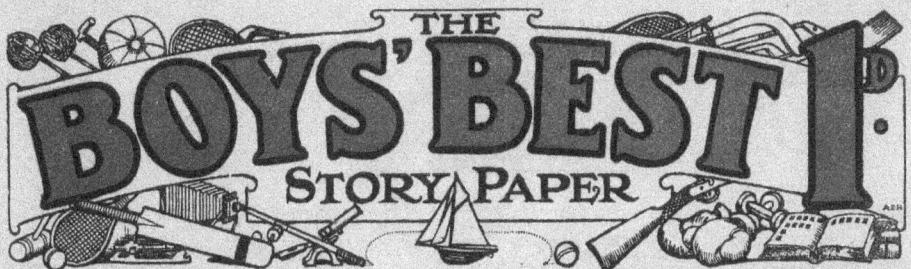

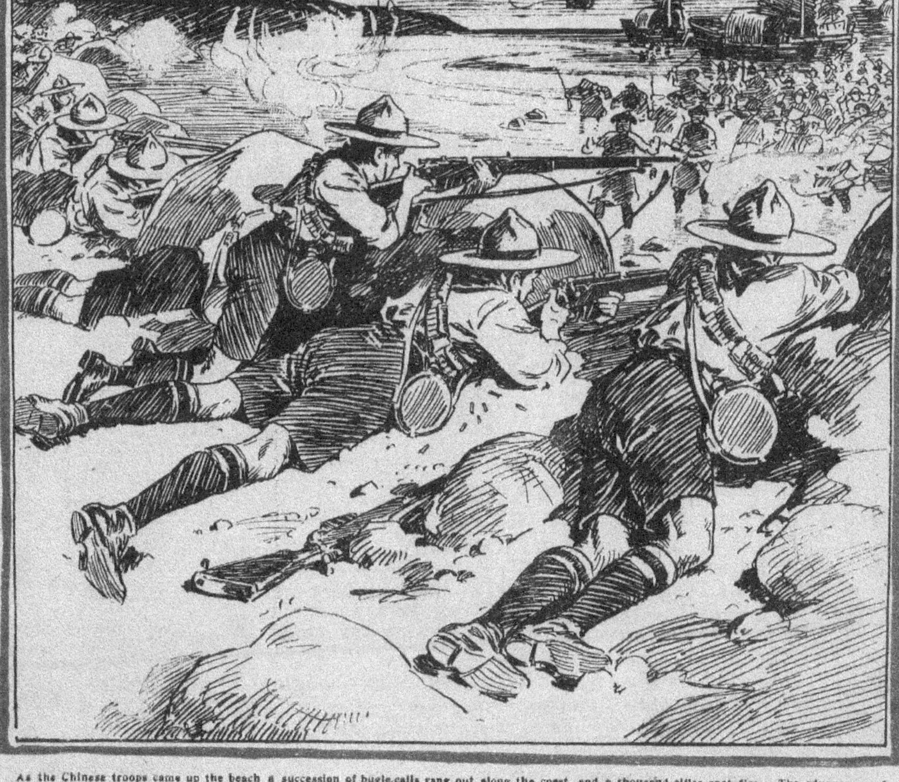

As the Chinese troops came up the beach a succession of bugle-calls rang out along the coast, and a thousand rifles spat fire. The advance guard of the Boy Scout army was there to resist the yellow invaders to the death!

THE MONGOLIAN MILLENIUM
"At Honolulu, smallpox, introduced by recently-arrived Chinese, is decimating the island" — *Daily Paper*
"About 1800 Chinese have, during the last few weeks, arrived at Sydney" — *Daily Paper*, April 14th.
"Crusader, from Hong Kong. Passengers: 200 Chinese" — *Evening News*, April 20th.
"From the Palmer Goldfield, which was, even after its 'Golden Days' capable of paying handsome wages for many years to two thousand white men, the Chinese have almost completely driven out white labour" — *Queensland Paper*.
"The Bulletin", 1881.

1908:

> Colonist [sic] statesmen have recently been all having a hack at the "Yellow Peril" question. The latest to consider it publicly is Premier Sir John Ward of New Zealand, in a speech made during the discussion of the reception of the U.S Fleet at Auckland. He predicted that some day there would be a fight to decide whether the white races or those of the East were to govern Australia, New Zealand, and the other islands of the Pacific. [45]

The Japanese came closest to fulfilling this prediction when they bombed Darwin in Australia on February 19th 1942. Fifty-four land based bombers and about one hundred and eighty eight attack aircraft were launched from four Japanese aircraft carriers in the Timor Sea. To quote from a National Archives of Australia web site:

> In the first attack, which began just before 10.00am, heavy bombers pattern-bombed the harbour and town; dive bombers escorted by Zero fighters then attacked shipping in the harbour, the military and civil aerodromes, and the hospital at Berrimah. The attack ceased after about 40 minutes. The second attack, which began an hour later, involved high altitude bombing of the Royal Australian Air Force base at Parap which lasted for 20-25 minutes. The two raids killed at least 243 people and between 300 and 400 were wounded. Twenty military aircraft were destroyed, eight ships at anchor in the harbour were sunk, and most civil and military facilities in Darwin were destroyed.

Later in the War other towns in northern Australia were bombed by the Japanese namely Townsville, Katherine, Wyndham, Derby, Broome and Port Holland. [10]

Apart from this story, reporting on the `Yellow Peril` in Hong Kong newspapers in the years sampled of 1905, 1908 and 1912 was very sparse. (There was an earlier report in the *South China Morning Post* for March 3rd 1908: `The yellow peril has raised itself in the South Seas - in the island of Tahiti,....The Avenir du Tonkin publishes some curious particulars of how Chinese are gaining mastery there, despite the fact that it is a French possession. [46]) This is surprising as it might be thought that Hong Kong had most to fear from a `Yellow Peril`, being so close to China. The *Overland China Mail* for February 21st 1905 picked up *The Times'*s opinion of the previous month, that Russia was more of a threat to the West, than Japan and that China was hostile to Japan.

The political climate in China at the time was as follows: In 1897, there was a "scramble for concessions" in China by the Great Powers including Germany, as the Chinese Empire seemed to disintegrate. In 1897 Germany seized Tsingtao and imposed a ninety-nine year lease on China, ceding the Shantung peninsula, which was rich in minerals. In the summer of 1898, the British gained a ninety-nine year lease on a part of Kwangtung province neighbouring Hong Kong, which became known as the New Territories. Even after ten years the New Territories seemed a strange place to the British culturally, judging from stories in the *South China Morning Post*, such as on the legality of the "unicorn dance", a kind of dance using lion masks today.

For some time the inadequacies of the defences of Hong Kong had been considered by the Government.....It was felt that the adequate defence of Hong Kong required not only the absolute control of the

---

(10) This information about northern Australian towns bombed and the details of the February 1942 attack on Darwin in the paragraph immediately above are from the National Archives of Australia Fact sheet 195-The bombing of Darwin web site: http://www.naa.gov.au/about-us/publications/fact-sheets/fs195.aspx

waters between the island of Hong Kong and the mainland but also the command of the northern and southern shores flanking the Lyemun Pass. [47]

In 1899 the U.S. Secretary of State, Hay, had sent a note to the other great powers such as Britain, France and Germany, advocating the maintenance of the open door policy in China. In those days this was not a euphemism for maintaining diplomatic relations. It meant that China's doors should be kept open for international trade. This soon led to moves towards the partition of China. Russia acquired the Liao Tung Peninsula with Port Arthur and Manchuria and Britain acquired Wei-hei-wei.

This drastic change in China's image, therefore, occurred because of the political crises in the Far East between c.1895 and c.1910, and on account of a certain amount of social insecurity about the Chinese, within Western countries. Other crises in addition to the above included the 1900 Boxer Uprising and the 1904-5 Russo-Japanese War. However none of these crises seriously affected Western dominance in China. The West, Japan and Russia had never been more powerful, when the `Yellow Peril` fear was on the rise. As has been written, 'The old Napoleonic image of a `sleeping giant` was to be revived, ironically at a time when European and American imperialism was at its zenith.` [48] The same author believes that the `Yellow Peril` presented an image of a lesser civilisation destroying a superior one, rather like the manner in which the Barbarians destroyed Rome. These images, combined with that of the Chinese opium addict and corrupter of females, through inter-marriage in the docklands of Cardiff, Liverpool and London (all part of the `Yellow Peril` myth,) were part of the potent racist imagery of one hundred years ago.

Obviously the genesis of the `Yellow Peril` image, cannot be dated to exactly 1895. This image had its roots in many different areas, within British politics and literature. By the beginning of the twentieth century, Limehouse and the whole riverside district of East London, stretching along the Thames from the Tower and Wapping, to Limehouse and inland north up to the Commercial Road, was a notorious slum area. Its streets of little terraced houses, were squeezed among canals and railway lines, timber yards and sawmills, lead-works and coal-yards, dry-docks, ship-repair yards, factories and workshops. There was heavy pollution and bad sanitation. There was overcrowding, along with low and irregular wages, among the highest levels of child mortality and the highest levels of poverty in London. [49]

An article in the `English Illustrated Magazine` of July 1900, just before the Boxer Uprising, which was surprisingly favourable towards the Chinese community of East London, put it this way:

> The English people of the neighbourhood give the Celestials an excellent character for peacefulness and quietness. There is seldom, or never, any quarrelling between them and their neighbours. Occasionally rows occur among the Celestials themselves, but in that case the English do not interfere, but let them settle it alone. [50]

Furthermore: 'Taken altogether....the Chinaman in Limehouse is a most peaceable, inoffensive, harmless character.` [51] No mention here of the Yellow Peril whatsoever.

Table 1 on the next page shows the Chinese population of London between 1881 and 1931 [11]

A famous literary image is that of Fu Manchu, or *The Mystery of Fu Manchu* (1913) by Arthur Henry Ward (`Sax Rohmer`.) Fu Manchu was an evil Chinese genius intent on paving the way for the destruc-

---

[11] This table is taken from Dr J.Seed`s web site and reproduced with permission, The Chinese in Limehouse 1900-1940 Untold London http://www.untoldlondon.org.uk/archives/TRA43336.html

Date	National	London	Limehouse
1881	224	109	70
1891	767	302	82
1901	387	120	55
1911	1120	247	101
1921	2419	711	101
1931	1934	1194	167

Table 1. Chinese population of London 1881-1931

tion of the white race. The image at the end of this chapter, closely parallels the idea of Fu Manchu. It is from the front cover of *The Yellow Danger* by M.P. Shiel (1898) ; in 1911:

An influential U.S. religious figure, G.G Rupert... published *The Yellow Peril*; or, *Orient vs. Occident*. Based on the phrase "the Kings from the East" in the Christian scriptural verse Revelation 16:12 [12], Rupert, who believed in the doctrine of British Israelism, claimed that China, India, Japan and Korea were attacking England and the U.S. , but that Jesus Christ would stop them. [52]

Rohmer published several other novels between 1915 and 1920, covering the dangerous Oriental presence in the London docks and drug smuggling. Edgar Wallace's 1926 novel *The Yellow Snake*, had Fing Su as its Fu Manchu character `and an underground Chinese network in London.` [53] Agatha Christie's *The Big Four* in 1927 featured another diabolical Chinese genius.

George Formby had his first record success in 1932, with `Chinese Laundry Blues`, recorded with the famous *Jack Hylton Orchestra*. It was a comical song about a lovesick Mr Wu in his Limehouse laundry.

> Oh Mr Wu
> What shall I do,
> I'm feeling kind of Limehouse Chinese Laundry Blues. [54]

It is worth quoting quite extensively from the above cited web site, by Dr John Seed in order to gain an insight into the status of the Chinese community, in London with regards to its population:

> By comparison with European immigrants the Chinese presence in Britain was negligible. The Chinese before the First World War numbered half of one percent of the foreign-born population of Britain. In the 1920s and 1930s they constituted just over one per cent. Compare the 1,194 Chinese aliens in Greater London in 1931, for instance, with over 25,000 Poles, nearly 18,000 Russians, 11,000 Italians, and over 9,000 French and Germans. [55]

Within London there was a marked concentration of Chinese in Limehouse. Around forty per cent of the Chinese counted in the pre-1914 censuses of London were in and around a couple of Limehouse streets. [56]

> "00.By the nineteen-twenties there were significant numbers [of Chinese] in several core West End boroughs – Westminster (75), St Pancras (65), St.Marylebone (38), together adding up to 25¢ of the Chinese in London. They were also settled in smaller numbers in such suburbs as Hampstead (31), Kensington (22), and Wandsworth (18)." [57]

By the early 1930s the largest settlement of the Chinese was in the West End: Kensington (135), Westminster (115), St Pancras (93), Paddington (75), Holborn (68) There were also sizeable clusters further out in Wandsworth (82), Hampstead (81), Hendon (44) and Ealing (34).[58]

These bare statistics can cover up the daily events of life within the Chinese community of London in the first few decades of the twentieth century. ` We can track the development of some kind of émigré Chi-

---

Revelation 16:12: Then the sixth [angel] emptied his bowl on the mighty river Euphrates , and its water was dried up to make ready a road for [the coming of] the Kings of the East (from the rising sun.) *The Amplified Bible* (Grand Rapids: Zondervan Publishing House,1987) p.1163

nese community. Its cafes, shops, and lodging-houses were places to meet and exchange news and gossip.' [59] But returning to the nature of China town at the end of the nineteenth century:

Chinatown, an 1895 article in the *Gentleman's Magazine* accurately stated, was no more than a single street of shops and boarding-houses: It exists by and for the Chinese firemen, seamen, stewards, cooks, and carpenters who serve on board the steamers plying between China and the port of London. [60]

The Chinese community of Limehouse was not a homogenous community set apart by itself. Also the size of this Chinese population, (see Table 1 above), created a negative impression in some areas of literature, which in quality and quantity far outweighed the small scale of the Chinese population in London. Limehouse was linked to the dangers to white women from Chinese and the use of opium. The true situation was as follows:

From the 1890s through to the 1950s the Chinese were a small minority in a mixed community of tradesman, casual labourers and transient sailors. Chinese boarding-houses and shops and cafes existed side by side with English working-class families, pubs, shops and tradesmen and a multinational population catering for sailors of a hundred different nations. [61]

Community relationships between Chinese workers and their British counterparts were not always calm:

Tensions exploded in the London Docks in 1908 when British seamen repeatedly stopped Chinese crews from signing on at the Board of Trade offices at East India Dock Road, a few hundred yards from the streets of `Chinatown.' [62]

Anti-Chinese unrest broke out again in the vicinity of Limehouse in May and June 1919 due to reports that Chinese seamen were signing on to work for much lower wages than British sailors were prepared to accept:

Antagonism in the London docks to the Chinese as cheap labour was exacerbated by conflicts over housing. There was an acute housing shortage in the area. In June 1919 a crowd attacked a house in Poplar into which two Chinese men and their English wives were moving. [63]

It may be instructive to establish what a key commentator on Chinese affairs, J.O.P. Bland, was saying about the `Yellow Peril` in 1912. He identified its cause as China's weakness and the resultant outflow of Chinese humanity:

In the present ferment of iconoclasm, and all its resultant lawlessness, lies the real Yellow Peril - for a weak and disorganised China means the danger of chronic unrest in the Far East....America and Australia have felt, and geared themselves against, the menace of this pressure of seething humanity. [64]

It is possible that these images were tied up with that of the "danger" and strange difference of the Chinese. Witness the parallels with the fears expressed in the *South China Morning Post* in 1908 and *The Boys Best Story Paper* in 1911. (See above.) Finally, there are other connotations to the word "Yellow" than "Oriental." Obviously yellow is an attempt to describe an East Asian person's skin. An early use of the word "yellow" in the English language actually meant "jealous" rather than cowardly: Yellow. To look yellow; to be jealous. I happened to call on Mr Green, who was out: on coming home, and finding me with his wife, he began to look confounded blue, and was, I thought, a little yellow. [65]

"Yellow" can mean0 cowardly and also sickly. It can also remind the reader of China as a place or circumstance of the exotic. In 1977 a *Dr Who* series featured `The Talons of Weng-Chiang` an evil genius who helps a time traveller. As late as the 1980s a popular British magazine, *Fortean Times* a journal dedicated to the description of anomalous phenomena from around the world was using the phrase 'Tales from The Yellow Emporium' to report strange events from China. For example issue 30 contained the following item:

> 'The Hairy Boy of China:' They called him Zhenhuan, meaning 'shock the universe', and the kid has indeed created something of a stir. Western journalists have handled his story in the usual degrading fashion, calling him 'monkey-boy', 'wolf-boy', 'freak', 'mutant'☐.but to the Chinese he is simply mao hai, a hairy child. [66]

Issue 33 of *Fortean Times* commented upon yet more Chinese exotica:

> 'Horny Dilemma': According to most reports☐an 88 year old woman of Hebei Province grew 2 horns on top of her head, some 6 months previously. The larger of the horns was said to be a quarter inch long, yellowish-brown and without feeling. [67]

This honesty about Western prejudice would have been refreshing in the era of Victorian Orientalism. According to the internet based Wikipedia, the free encyclopaedia:

Yellow Peril (sometimes Yellow Terror) was a phrase, that originated in the late 19th century with greater immigration of Chinese and Japanese labourers to various Western countries, notably the United States. The term, a colour metaphor for race refers to the skin colour of east Asians, and the fear that the mass immigration of Asians threatened white wages, standards of living and indeed, civilization itself. The phrase "yellow peril" was common in the newspapers owned by William Randolph Hearst. [68]

In symbolism, the word yellow also means treacherous, jealous, inconstant, and adulterous. All these would be additional ways of demonising the Chinese through the medium of, say, children's comics, and there was certainly the innuendo in the more serious provincial press, that there was a danger of sexual immorality on the side of the Chinese. This last point comes closest to adultery and referred to the Chinese males' alleged habit of preferring white females, as partners for marriage. The significant factor about the 'Yellow Peril' scare was its far-ranging emphasis. It stretched from seamen in Liverpool, concerned that Chinese seamen were undercutting white labour, by working for lower wages, to international geopolitics. The same fear of foreign races was prevalent in the mid-1920s, as can be seen in F. Scott Fitzgerald's *The Great Gatsby,* first published in 1926:

> " Civilization's going to pieces, " broke out Tom violently. " I've gotten to be a terrible pessimist about things. Have you read The Rise of the Coloured Empires by this man Goddard?.....Well, it's a fine book, and everybody ought to read it. The idea is if we don't look out the white race will be - will be utterly submerged. It's all scientific stuff; its been proved "

Two other components of the 'Yellow Peril' were Chinese overpopulation and their potential capacity for industrial competition. Both these two factors were not necessarily occurring in the late-nineteenth to early-twentieth century. They were just scares, serious ones nevertheless. 'It is clear that fears about excessive fertility played a part in forming Victorian notions about the Chinese.....while the Chinese character presented some problems, inscrutability being particularly resented , as it was in the Hindu.' [70] The 'Yellow Peril' was always more a feature of the imagination than a real problem. There was never a real danger of China and Japan uniting and threatening the West. The two countries were militarily, politically and economically incompatible. The "problem" of Chinese seamen in British ports was exaggerated, their mere presence being turned into a problem. By the mid-1920s, as far as Sino-British relationships are concerned, the `Yellow Peril` had turned into the `Red Peril`. Chapter Eight looks at this in more detail. The following chapter looks at the issue of the `Yellow Peril` scare in the United States.

CHAPTER SIX
The Yellow Peril Scare and the United States of America

Chinese immigration into the United States dates from the early nineteenth century onwards. The `Yellow Peril` scare in the U.S. turned out to be more damaging to relationships between the Chinese immigrant group and their host country's population, than in Britain. Historian Stuart Creighton Miller observed, for example, that Chinese immigrants were ` considered by most persons as very contemptible.....cunning and corrupt, treacherous and vindictive, [given] to lechery, dishonesty, xenophobia, cruelty, despotism, filth and intellectual inferiority.` [1]   By the 1850s Chinese immigrants on the West coast of the U.S. were working on railway track manufacture, prospecting for gold and labouring on agricultural projects. Also in this decade, apart from the immigration into California:

> `..Many more were going to Washington State and to Oregon and to the Deep South in fact: Mississippi and Alabama in the United States.`[2]

`By....1851 there were 25,000 Chinese working in California.` [3] The Chinese, escaping from poverty and unrest in China, faced fierce opposition from native white Americans, because it was feared that the low paid Chinese were undercutting the latter's wages. In 1862 88 Chinese were killed in violence relating to competition with whites. On occasion anti-Chinese feelings in the U.S. spilled over into violence such as in the coal mines of Rock Springs, Wyoming in 1885 when 28 Chinese mine workers `were killed in a mass attack.` [4] White Americans appeared to overlook the fact that the Chinese fought for their adopted but divided country on both sides of the bitter separation during the American Civil War (1861-1865.) By the 1880s, American trade unions had successfully campaigned against Chinese immigration. In 1882 the U.S. Congress passed the Chinese Exclusion Act. This Act was passed, as a result of the belief amongst trade unions that Chinese immigrants, particularly in California, were basically coolies or virtually slave labour ` whose presence degraded American labour.` [5]

Around 1880 Chinese workers were active in the service trades, mining and casual labour outside of California. A writer in `The Forum` in 1888 claimed that Chinese labour ` has tended to the enrichment of the capitalists.` The Act banned the immigration of Chinese labour for ten years. By 1890 the various acts of legislation had created a huge imbalance of the population of male to female Chinese, to the order of males to females of 27:1. For more than 50 years old Chinese men always outnumbered the young.

The Act was renewed for another ten years in 1892 and in 1902 the ban became permanent. This legislation was repealed in 1943, when the U.S. government allowed only a small quota, of 105 Chinese immigrants a year. This partial repeal of the legislation, was due to the help China gave to America in the fight against Japan during World War Two. So Chinese immigrants were restricted from the late nineteenth century, into the early twentieth century and ended up living in enclaves or China towns. (One such China town was in Honolulu in Hawaii where bubonic plague and a devastating fire in January 1900 alienated the Chinese residents from their white and Japanese compatriots because of supposed injustices. In the 1880s tension between Chinese merchants and their white counterparts emerged over the latter's plan to control the competition from the Chinese by trying to limit their moving from agriculture to business. Furthermore white Americans in Hawaii in the medical profession were suspicious of Chinese and Japanese immigrants because they were thought to be from places where disease was to be found. Concerning the travel ban between locations in Hawaii:

Reflecting the internationally held opinion that Asian races were more susceptible to bubonic plague than other races, and hence more likely to be its carriers, both the inter-island [travel] ban and the Honolulu city ban were absolute for Chinese and Japanese residents. [6]

Tension rose between the Chinese community in Hawaii and whites over the medical authorities plan to cremate victims of the plague. Whilst whites praised the plan, the Chinese were upset because cremation raised the prospect of spiritual oblivion. Also, when an attempt to burn down a part of Chinatown's plague infested buildings got out of control, destroying a large part of Chinatown, some Chinese were understandably irate. `In vague terms, they warned of reprisal and retribution, perhaps when China rose again to world power or when the perpetrators of the great fire faced their God in the life hereafter.` [7] A similar risk of the whole scale burning of the Chinatown in San Francisco arose in March 1900 after the detection of bubonic plague. However the threat was lifted after legal measures were taken. Tourists were guided around these places and shown fake opium dens and other imagined paraphernalia of the `wicked Orientals`. The great San Francisco earthquake of April 1906 facilitated Chinese immigration for a while. Official records of Chinese incomers, were destroyed in the fire which followed the earthquake, so would-be Chinese immigrants invented genealogies which "proved" they had relatives in California. The Chinese arriving at the immigration office on Angel Island Processing Centre, off the coast of California were asked up to one thousand questions ` to be corroborated by those on the mainland to whom they were supposedly related. [8] Conditions on Angel Island were poor, but there was nothing the Chinese immigrants could do except wait there. Jack London, in his novel of early twentieth century love and labour in post 1906 San Francisco earthquake California, *The Valley of the Moon*, first published in October 1913, comments on the situation with regards to Chinese labour in California. In the following extract, Mr Gunston, a commission merchant, is talking to Billy and his wife Saxon about Chinese entrepreneurial skills:

> "..in a year more, out of the three shares, he organized a company of his own. One year of this, with bad luck, and he just broke even. That brings it up to three years ago. The following year, bumper crops, he netted four thousand. The next year it was five thousand. And last year he cleaned up nineteen thousand dollars. Pretty good, eh, for old broken-down Chow Lam? [9]

Later Billy, the hero of the novel, shows forth the racism of native Americans towards Chinese immigrants. Mr Gunston has been telling Billy and Saxon about hard working Sing Kee, " the potato King of Stockton." [10] Billy says: `An him a Chink…..They ought to be some new country for us white folks to go to.` Gunston goes on to state that Chinese are honest and keep their word. Finally Billy comments on all the differences between " Chinks" and Americans, by saying: ` What does a Chink do? Work his damned head off. That's all he's good for.` [11] A later story by Jack London, The *Unparalled Invasion* (1914) taking pace in a fictional 1975, describes China as taking over its neighbours and with ultimate intent the entire planet due to its increasing population.

> 'H.P.Lovecraft was in constant fear of Asiatic culture engulfing the world, and a few of his stories reflect this, such as The Horror At Red Hook, where "slant eyed immigrants practice nameless rites in honor of heathen gods by the light of the moon" and He, where the protagonist is given a glimpse of the future – the "yellow men" have conquered the world, and now dance to their drums over the ruins of the white man.[12]

Ian Buruma states: "….the modern idea of yellow peril is commonly ascribed to the Americans. The influx of Chinese immigrants, in the late 19th century , provoked fears of economic competition….. heathenism, and racial pollution. He (Kaiser Wilhelm II of Germany) was obsessed by it (the yellow peril.) He sent ferocious messages to his cousin Nicky the Russian tsar, urging him to defend the borders of civilization against " the yellow danger." [13]

Between 1906 and 1907 the first major economic boycott of United States by the Chinese of American goods took place but this did not stop America influence within China up until the Communist take over of power in 1949. From about the late 1920s onwards there was an influence of America missionary activity in China with the Y.M.C.A. and the Y.W.C.A. introducing technical knowledge and primary and college level education. By the 1930s and 1940s the phrase `Yellow Peril` had been transferred to the Japanese in the face of their aggressive expansion in China and the Pacific. After World War Two, when Japanese-Americans were released from internment there was a movement by this ethnic group away from the West coast to urban areas, thus lessening the competition with whites. `In the 1980s the Yellow Peril concept was revived as the U.S .was in intense competition with Japan over industrial supremacy. The beating (to) death of Chinese-American Vincent Chin in 1982 outside Detroit by U.S. auto workers was a hate crime motivated by fear of Asian economic competition.` [14]

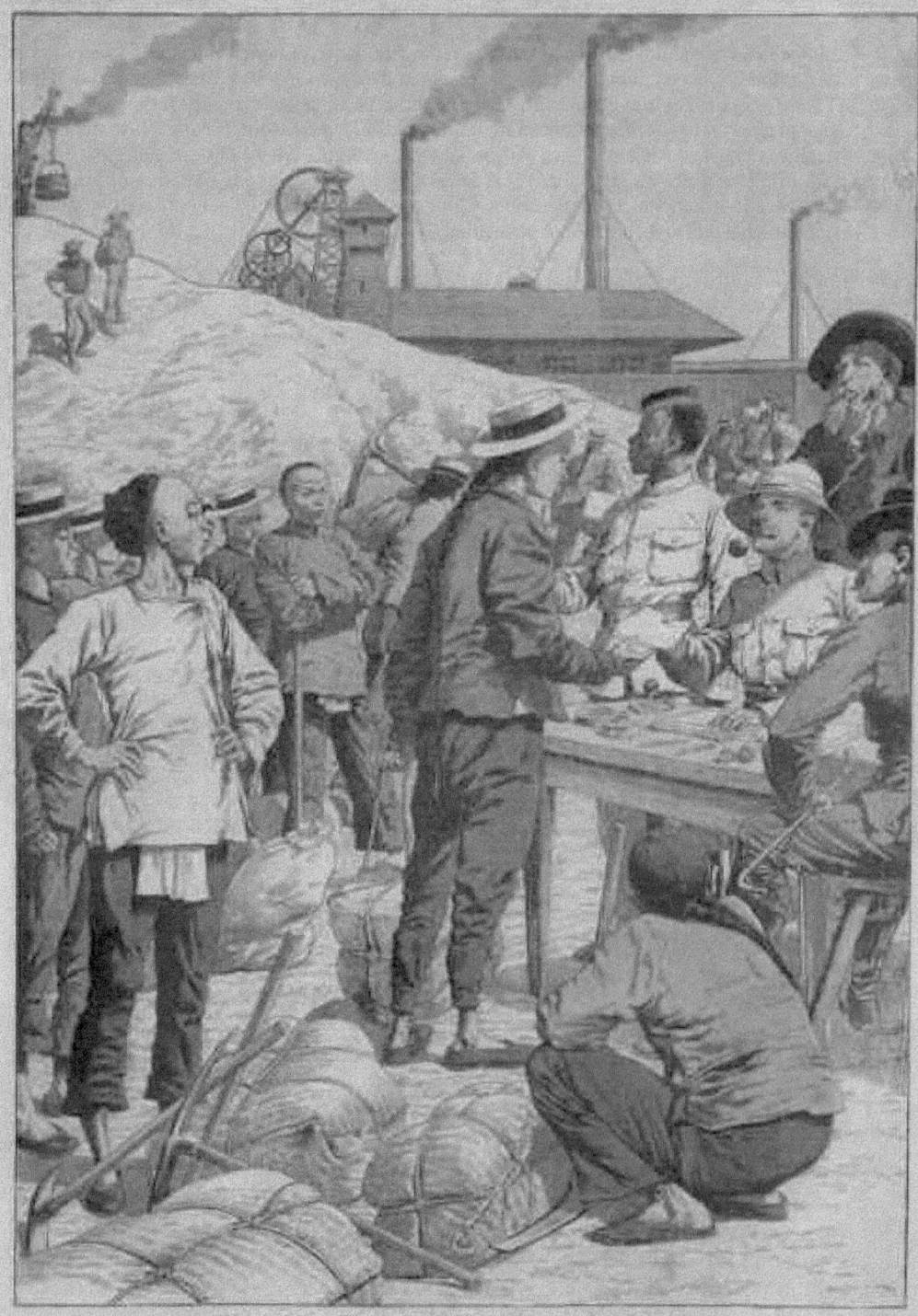

DANS L'AFRIQUE DU SUD
Travailleurs chinois s'engageant dans les mines

CHAPTER SEVEN
Chinese indentured labour in South Africa

By the time of the end of the first South African (Boer) War (1899-1902) the Rand economy, once thriving, was devastated, with an urgent need to restart mining production because the gold mines had virtually ceased functioning. At this point in time, Chinese workers were employed all over the world on railway construction, in mines and on road works:

In contrast to the European, Indian and African unskilled labourers, the Chinese were recruited not only because they were `industrious` and `cheap,` [1] but because they were preferred since they were regarded as more docile, submissive and obedient. [2] These traits featured prominently in almost all pro-Chinese labour lobbies world-wide, and the Witwatersrand (Rand) capitalist campaign to obtain Chinese labourers for the gold mines at the turn of this century was no exception. [3]

In fact, the Chinese labourers on the Rand were not as passive as received wisdom suggests. Chinese workers `resisted the exploitation of the capitalist system by all the means at their disposal.` [4]

By the turn of the twentieth century, the Chinese population in South Africa was below 5000 whilst in the U.S. A the figure was 100,000.

Very small numbers of Chinese immigrants arrived in the Cape Colony (South Africa) from the late seventeenth century and in the U.S. from the late eighteenth century [from China.] They were generally individual males who came ashore from passing ships or might have migrated intentionally. They were mostly occupied as merchants and small-scale traders, with a lesser number of labourers and servants..... at the Cape there were...convicts or ex-convicts who had been banished by the Dutch East India Company in Batavia. The latter were of generally little consequence as they left once their sentences expired.
[5]

The number of Chinese in South Africa during this period never exceeded about 50. In the 1860s and the 1870s diamonds and then gold were discovered in South Africa and this, combined with the very poor socio-economic situation in China led to the immigration of Chinese labour into South Africa, or more specifically the Rand in the Transvaal. White labour was 'unable to find satisfactory employment' at the end of the Boer War and by May 1903 'half the stamps at the mines were idle, because only 50,000 Kafirs are procurable when 150,000 men are required.' [6] This lead to a situation in which Rand capitalists hoped that public opinion would demand even Chinese labour, although it was so unpopular, despite the South African trading population being so against indentured Chinese labour. From 1904, 63,695 Chinese indentured labourers were contracted to work on the Rand gold mines after a successful campaign by the above mentioned Rand capitalists and local British authorities. 'Although the indentured contract system introduced in South Africa regulated conditions and treatment, the Chinese were still subjected to flagrant abuses by both fellow mine workers and management.' [7]

A document [8] held in the National Archives, London, shows a proposal by British authorities in London to provide food, etc on board ships transporting Chinese labour to South Africa. Table 2 below shows the type and amount of provisions that Chinese migrants were allowed in early 1904., adapted from this document.

For every passenger per diem:- Rice or bread stuffs	Not less than 1 1/3lb
Dried (and) or salt fish	1/3 lb
Chinese condiments and curry-stuffs	1 oz
Fresh vegetables, such as sweet potatoes, turnips, carrots, and pumpkins	1 1/3 lb
Firewood	2lb
Water(to be carried in tanks or sweet casks)	1 gallon

Table 2. Provisions allowed by Chinese migrants to South Africa in 1904

In South Africa (as in the United States) the Chinese were seen by whites as unfair competitors in the employment market because they were prepared to work for lower wages and accept a lower standard of living and also because they excelled in profitable sectors. The imperial powers generally believed that ' no race in the world would do them better service than the Chinese.' [9] In fact: as author Lynn Pan has argued about the U.S., but which is equally applicable to South Africa and elsewhere:

Middle-class Chinese immigrants were up against the fact that because the first Chinese to enter America had been labourers, in the ordering of (foreign) minorities, ethnic Chinese had been assigned a low place in American minds. [10]

In the first decade of the twentieth century Chinese indentured labour and the Chinese already resident in South Africa were a major issue on three counts:

First, in the Cape elections of 1902, which culminated in the introduction of the Cape Exclusion Act; second, the British elections of 1906, when the Liberal government defeated the Conservatives and then had to follow through on promises to repatriate the indentured Chinese on the South African mines; and third, in the 1907 local Transvaal responsible government , when the Het Volk and Labour parties successfully joined forces also to terminate the Chinese indenture system on the gold-mines.[11]

In a communication with me in November 2007 Harris said: 'There was indeed a "yellow peril" scare in South Africa-in fact it played amongst others a key role in the elections of 1907 when the Het Volk party came to power in the Transvaal Colony.' [12]

In 1906 the Liberal government in England and in 1907 the Het Volk government in the Transvaal passed legislation prohibiting recruitment and preventing the right to contract renewal. [13] Repatriation began in mid-1907 and by the end of the decade all Chinese mine labourers had left South Africa. Whilst these discriminatory legislative acts were being ordained, the Chinese community beyond the miners felt increasingly under siege. Along with Mahatma Ghandi, they resisted the servility imposed upon them by the precursor to apartheid. 'Gandhi often praised the Chinese for their solidarity and steadfast determination during the resistance struggle, and commended their exemplary role to the Indians.' [14]

White communists and socialists were of no help to Chinese mine labourers. As Harris has also stated:

> The trade unionism on the Rand at this time was still very much of the "old unionism" type, adhering to craft protection-there was obviously no communism at this time and the socialist and syndicalist movements were only just beginning to feature. The early "socialism" that began to form during the first decade of the twentieth century upheld the slogan of "white workers of the world unite"- and thus there was very little regard for the Chinese, who were in fact seen as the "enemy" that the Rand capitalist had brought in to undermine their positions even further. [15]

CHAPTER EIGHT
The Red Peril:
The British and the Rise of Communism in China

By the mid 1920s the British, in their colonies and concessions in China, particularly Hong Kong and Shanghai, were facing what one newspaper perceived to be " The World's Greatest Peril", (according to a pamphlet of the Shanghai *North China Daily News* in 1926 or 1927) namely Bolshevism. The rise of Communism in China can be attributed, in part, to the failure of the West, to appeal to China's young intelligentsia after 1917. Various other events, such as the Bolsheviks decision to annul the Tsar's territorial claims in China and the failure of the Treaty of Versailles in 1919 to stop imperialism in China were significant. The American President Wilson's public relations business spread the word of the rights of self-determination for countries such as China and elsewhere but this amounted to nothing for China in 1919.

In the aftermath of World War One, the Paris Peace Conference rewarded Japan's support for the allies in the Far East by granting her the former German territory of Kiaochow. Undoubtedly the success of the Bolshevik revolution in its overthrow of an outdated system of government, had an impact on young Chinese intellectuals. Also, on May 4th 1919 there were student demonstrations in Peking, to protest against the poor treatment of China in the post World War One Paris peace talks. These demonstrations heralded a period of intellectual debate and liberal thinking in China called the May 4th Movement. This opened up the minds of certain individuals to Marxism and Leninism. One of the first Communists was Li Ta-chao. He was a librarian at Peking National University. So was Mao who was converted to Marxism under the influence of Li`s Marxist Research Society founded in 1918. Li was attracted to Communism as a way of harnessing national patriotism and restoring the greatness of China on which the more competent powers of the West had so ruthlessly trampled.` Ironically national pride was again harnessed to encourage the greatness of China in events such as the 2008 Beijing Olympics, which opened up China to capitalism and stirrings towards democracy.

Further influences for the rise of Chinese Communism, were the failure of attempts at parliamentary democracy since 1912 and the poverty and oppression of the poor in factories and villages. In 1921 the Chinese Communist Party was founded. By 1925 the Party was in a strong position with workers and students in Shanghai and Canton. According to Jerome Ch'en (Mao and the Chinese Revolution London: Oxford University Press, 1967 p.100) Chinese Communist Party membership rose from 1000 in May 1925 to 10,000 six months later and Communist youth corps from 2000 in May to 9,000 in September. On May 30th 1925 there began the most renowned series of strikes in modern Chinese history. The background to this was the killing of a factory worker on May 15th, during a clash between management and workers at the number seven cotton mill in Shanghai. This was a Japanese-owned mill. The British police were involved in the incident because the factory was situated in the International Settlement.

A number of workers were arrested by the police in an attempt to restore calm. In the following fortnight students and workers gathered their forces, and on May 30th there was a large demonstration of about two thousand people, down the Nanking Road , threatening to "give themselves up", i.e. be arrested at the Louza Police station. When the marchers began to manhandle the police, the police opened fire killing between four and forty people depending on which account is read. The killings sparked off a general strike in the foreign settlements in June, and during the strike a Shanghai Cotton Mill Union was organized under Communist leadership. The business community, represented by the General Chamber of Commerce, lent its support to the demonstrations planned for May 30th in protest against new laws proposed in April, which would make traditional Chinese business practices more difficult. Such as the introduction of child labour laws. So the interests of Shanghai`s proletariat and bourgeoisie coincided in the May 30th Movement. The British media were concerned with the part the Communists played in the Movement. It has been said in a letter written to me by a researcher in this subject that:

My own research – including work on Shanghai Municipal Police activities and thinking- would not suggest that Chinese communism was much of an issue for Britons before May 30. However, Shanghai, as a conduit for Russian refugees, was seen as a possible route for `bolshevik agitators` to come through on their way to British and European possessions in S.E. Asia[2]

The basis of British media thinking in 1925, was that the Chinese were incapable of independent political mass action and thus needed an external source, namely the Bolsheviks, to lead them. Bolshevism itself was somehow "un-Chinese." According to The Times` The novel fact in this summer`s outbreak against certain classes of foreigner in China is that the discontent is being organized,taught, guided and directed by a type of foreigner who is in perpetual revolt against all the institutions of Europe....`[3] This `type of foreigner` was the Bolshevik, taking advantage of Chinese radicalism. A dissenting view came from the American journal Christian Century of 18th June 1925, `It is absurd to see in such an outburst as this only another evidence of the machinations of Moscow.....But all the Russian agents in the Far East could have done nothing had not the other foreign nations given them plenty of grievances on which to play.`[4]

In a semi-autobiograqphical novel of his stay in Shanghai as a refugee, circa 1926-1927, William Gawan Sewell, a former teacher at West China Union University,Chengdu, records a Pole,referring to the "agitators", ` But I dell you, dey are not Chinamen. Dey are Bolshevics!`[5] His speech happened at the multi-national boarding house Sewell was staying in. It indicates the Western belief, not only confined to the British, that to be a Communist was un-Chinese. But for the Chinese it was perhaps more of a case of the following, as recorded by Sewell elsewhere in the novel,(being a talk by a Chinese person) : `We do not want to have our old culture replaced by a poor copy of Western civilisation`[6] This same Sewell in

File 22, noted that the notorious sign in a Shanghai park did not say "No dogs or Chinese " but "Point One. The Gardens are reserved for the European Community. Point Four. Dogs and bicycles are not permitted."

It is important to remember that in 1924, the Labour Government lost power because of the red peril aroused by the Zinoviev Letter scare, so "red perils" would be relatively fresh in the minds of the newspaper reading public of Britain and the colonies. Paul Gillingham in his book At The Peak Hong Kong Between The Wars gives a survey of the events of the Hong Kong-Canton strike boycott:

Following the Hong Kong-Canton Strike Committee's announcement of a trade boycott against Hong Kong on 6 July 1925, pickets began searching all incoming ships at Canton for British goods or goods imported from Hong Kong and prevented all British ships and ships from Hong Kong from entering any Kwangtung port. The boycott was largely a response to an earlier attempt by Stubbs to impose a blockade on Canton. Stubbs had hoped to break Canton as a means of ending the strike in Hong Kong, but soon found that the only way of stopping foodstuffs and other goods entering Canton was by establishing a full naval blockade. With only a small fleet of ships at his disposal this proved to be impossible. The Canton boycott of Hong Kong was an entirely different matter. The only way Hong Kong merchants could trade with Canton was to ship their goods eight hundred miles to Shanghai and then south to Canton by train. [7]

However, 'The trans-shipment of textiles, rice and silk was, in the words of a prominent local dealer," literally dead." [8] Stubbs was the Governor of Hong Kong at the time. Stubbs a somewhat headstrong man wanted to send a military force to Canton to break the boycott by force. The Chinese business community in Hong Kong along with a reluctant Tung Wah Hospital raised enough money to fund a warlord army under a Cantonese general, Wei Bong-ping, to break the boycott. The attempted coup failed utterly. It was not until a new Governor, Sir Cecil Clementi who had a far greater understanding of the Chinese and their concept of "face" took over and the arrival of the Nationalist leader Chiang Kai-shek in Canton after another coup on March 20th 1926, that the boycott was lifted on October 10th 1926. By this time the influence of the left-wing radicals had declined in Canton.

But returning to the early days of the boycott: The Hong Kong Overland China Mail of July 30th 1925 reported on a public meeting in the local City Hall at which certain resolutions were passed:

Not in any spirit of antagonism to our ancient Chinese friends, but with the sincere belief that by the eradication of the Bolshevists from their midst lies not only the hope of international salvation in all dealings with China but the preservation of her own rights and (?) the country from utter destruction. [9]

By this time a general strike and boycott of British shipping, had engulfed Hong Kong and Canton, as mentioned above. This was sparked off by the Shameen Incident of June 23rd 1925. This involved the Kuomintang organizing fifty thousand workers to march on the foreign settlement at Shameen. This led to a confrontation in which gunfire was exchanged between the British and French marines, guarding the community and Chinese soldiers. Eighty-three people were killed and five hundred wounded. The strike and boycott of British trade which followed prevented British ships coming to Canton and caused businesses to languish in Hong Kong. This strike and boycott lasted until October 1926. During the strike, as if to emphasise the fear and isolation felt by the British in Hong Kong, the Governor Stubbs telegrammed an official in London, Amery, to state that the unrest, 'was unquestionably a communist conspiracy instigated and led by Russia' [10] (26/6/1925 CO 129/488. C.O. 34204.) Later he sent a memorandum to Amery stating that the 'Red Boxers' would attack the colony [11] (30/10/25 CO 129/489 CO 53914/25)

The fears of the British during the whole May 30th Movement and the associated events were varied. There was a fear the unrest would spread to other British possessions, such as India. There was a fear that if the communists were victorious in China this would lead to British-Russian rivalry. There was also a fear that the industrial unrest and boycott of British shipping would have a harmful affect on British exports to China. China was a major outlet for the Lancashire cotton mills, and at this time Britain had ten times the investments of the U.S.A. in China. Such was the impact of the unrest that, within a month of May 30th, a joint letter was sent by most of the major British firms in China, urging the Foreign Office to apologise for the deaths on May 30th.

It might seem that at this time it would be most unlikely to find any pro-British sentiment in Hong Kong at all. This is not the case however. At the end of May 1925, some gates were returned to the village of Kam Tin in the New Territories, from where they had been confiscated during the take over of the New Territories in 1898. They were confiscated as a reprisal for resistance to the takeover by the villagers of Kam Tin and sent back to the estate of the then Governor Sir Henry Blake in Ireland. In 1924 the villagers requested that the gates be sent back, and in 1925 Governor Sir Reginald Stubbs arranged for their return. In 1925, the British version of events as reported in *The South China Morning Post* of May 27th 1925 was given as follows by Mr Bird the Commodore, 'It was necessary at the time to remove the gates because the villagers, through ignorance, defied the Government: It is no longer necessary to hold them because the villagers of Kam Tin have proved their loyalty to the British flag and have prospered under British rule' [12] The same paper gives a translation of a village elders` song of praise to the British, part of which is reproduced here:

> Glorious Great Britain! Queen of all the Seas !
> Wide o`er your far flung Empire
> do your gracious acts extend.
> Your greatness and your goodness
> on every hand one sees
> To all your subjects` wishes a kindly ear you lend [13]

So, coming in the midst of all the agitation, unrest and anti-imperialism in China at the time, this is a very interesting anomaly. In fact Hong Kong itself can be said to have been an anomaly, with its survival as a colonial territory up to 1997 despite the proximity of a theoretically anti-imperialist regime. Despite Hong Kong`s commitment to the capitalist system, this never led to serious conflict with post-1949 China, (although in the 1960s small bombs occasionally exploded in Hong Kong`s commercial district planted by pro Red Guard elements influenced by events in Cultural Revolution wracked China. See Jon Downes`s account below.) Rather it can de argued that capitalism in Hong Kong benefited China, (remembering Deng Xiaoping's famous dictum that "it doesn't matter if the cat is black or white as long as it catches the mice" which some have interpreted as meaning that it doesn't matter if China employs communism or the market economy as long as the goods are delivered. Deng launched pro-market reforms in December 1978.) Hong Kong's way of life continued through the fall of the Manchu Dynasty in 1911, through the unrest and civil war in China in the 1920s and 1930s and the period of communism since 1949. The Red Peril threat Hong Kong faced forty one years after the early days of Communism in Canton came at the beginning of the Great Proletarian Cultural Revolution in China. Jon Downes, a friend of the author, remembers how the events across the border in China spilled over into Hong Kong when he was a child of about ten. In his book *The Island of Paradise* (not about Hong Kong but Puerto Rico): Downes comments:

> It is a little known fact that there were Red Guards in Hong Kong. There was a revolu-

tion in Hong in May 1967, and it was a revolution that very nearly succeeded! What are now known as the Hong Kong 1967 riots, but was in fact an attempt by the Peoples Republic of China to overthrow the Hong Kong Government , started in May 1967 when local communists turned a labour dispute in an artificial flower factory, into large scale demonstrations against the rule of the Gwai-Lo. [13]

On 8 July, Red Guards killed five policemen in a gun battle at the border town of Sha Tau Kok. Many years later my father told me that-together with the other senior members of ,HM Government, he had been called to a secret bunker below the Government Offices. There, he and his colleagues had been issued with side arms and told to expect an immanent invasion. In the event the invasion didn't happen There were lots of bomb threats. Real bombs, and even more decoys were planted throughout the colony. Laboratories in some leftist schools were turned into bomb making workshops..

I only saw one troop of Red Guards. They were marching up the Peak Road outside our flat and chanting something about Ho Chi Minh. [14]

The year before, in 1966, riots occurred in Kowloon, Hong Kong, ostensibly over the issue of a rise in ferry fares. Any Communist involvement was white washed in the official government report on the disturbances. Part of the conclusion to the report simply stated:

We do not believe that political, economic and social frustrations were the direct cause of the 1966 riots but within the economic and social fields there are factors, to which we have drawn attention and that need to be watched, lest they provide inflammable material which could erupt into disturbances should opportunity arise in the future. [15]

---

(13) *Gwai*-Lo is literally translated as `Foreign Devil` - That is, the British

CHAPTER NINE
Conclusion

Today, the Chinese are potentially a more realistic threat to Western and Japanese political and economic power than they have ever been over the last one hundred years. This is because of China's growing economic and political power since she opened up to tourism and investment from the West in the late 1970s. Materialism has replaced communism as the new prevailing ideology in early twenty-first century China. This is a far more subtle threat to the West and Japan than the blatant and largely fictitious `Yellow Peril` threat of 100 years ago. Another less blatant threat, but still serious and growing is the problem of pollution and global warming. If there is a `Yellow Peril` scare today it is hardly militaristic. There is no obvious military threat to the West from China, other than any threat to Western interests in Taiwan. There is no ideological threat from China. China is only nominally Communist and has no known plans to export revolution to other parts of the world.

According to *The Times* of December 20th 2004 ` Fear of China is gripping the world.` [1] In early December 2004, the sale of IBM's personal computer business to ` China's leading manufacturer, Lenovo` was described as ` a great leap forward for China, still nominally a communist country, onto the global business stage. `[2] If there is a `Yellow Peril` threat today, replacing Chinese disease or crime, it is China's economy and pollution. China's economic growth (its economy grew by 9% in 2005 and by 10.7% in 2006, see *The Guardian*, March 6th 2007:- `China edges towards a greener shade of red. [3]`), as represented by its investments in Sudan or Shanghai skyscrapers, is respected and perhaps feared by the U.S.A. and Japan.

In fact by the summer of 2008 most of Sudan's oil was being imported by China. China has also invested in Nigeria and Angola's railway network and almost half of a 754 mile highway in Algeria. China has offered $6 billion to Angola and has provided aid for the huge Mepanda Nkua dam in Mozambique. `Africa now supplies a third of China's crude oil imports` (*The Guardian* February 5th 2007. Thanks China, now go home: buy-up of Zambia revives old colonial fears. [4]) There is a significant Chinese presence in Zambia, a presence of least 2,300 people but possibly as high as tens of thousands. During a tour of Africa during late January and early February 2007 the Chinese president Hu Jintao gave out hundreds of millions of dollars in investments in Zambia. However, in 2005, around 50 Zambians were killed in an accident in an explosives factory that supplied a Chinese run copper mine. When in the summer of 2006 ` the main opposition leader in Zambia, infuriated by the deaths in the explosives factory, made Chinese investment an issue in the presidential election, the Chinese Embassy threatened to break off relations with Zambia if he were elected. Hardly a model of non-interference.` [5] According to the U.K. international development secretary Hilary Benn, speaking in February 2007: ` We need to talk more to China about how we can work together because we both have the same interests, which are the development of Africa as a continent. ` [6] (*The Guardian* February 8th 2007 Chinese aid to Africa may do more harm than good, warns Benn.) ` At a summit in Shanghai in May, [2007] Chinese leaders promised a further $20 billion to Africa, though it is unclear whether this is intended to take the form of aid or commercial loans.` [7] Also in May 2007, Marc Ravalomanana, the president of Madagascar told Chinese leaders in Shanghai, ` You are an example of transformation...... We in Africa must learn from your success....China now trains 3000 African officials a year. [8]

According to *The New York Times* August 18th 2007, there may have been up to 750,000 Chinese working in Africa. [9] In countries such as Sierra Leone and Liberia, small scale Chinese traders selling electronic goods and textiles have become established, some sleeping in their stalls at outdoor markets, opening their shops at dawn. Apart from computers, Chinese cars, kitchen appliances, televisions and computer games, are all beginning to make an impact on the world market. All this progress on China's part is gradually reversing the hegemony of the West. China's economic success is prompting Chinese people to migrate, to other parts of the world for education and employment. All this commitment by the Chinese to invest time and money beyond their shores is beginning to be matched by sending students in the West: `Just over 2000 [students] at this moment (i.e. May 2008) are preparing for their O Levels in Mandarin Chinese,` [10] so said the Sinologist Jonathan Spence in the Spring of 2008. He was referring to British students. The Chinese, along with Iranians, Eritreans and Somalis were among the largest group of asylum seekers in the U.K. in 2005,[11] This fuels heated debate about immigration, but so far this has not developed into a `Yellow Peril` scare. Chinese immigrants in the United Kingdom take the lowliest jobs such as cockle picking; in the north-west of England. One hundred years ago, Chinese immigrants were taking equally humble jobs; such as being laundry owners. There has been a Chinese presence in the U.K. for about 150 years, but the fantasies of the `Yellow Peril` scaremongers that China would take over the world, have never come true.

However, in some parts of the world immigration from China is again becoming a problem in the eyes of indigenous workers. In October 2004 irate Spanish cobblers fought with Chinese migrant workers from Wenzhou. The Spaniards feared losing their jobs to the Chinese. China insists that it is not a threat to anyone. In December 2005 China issued a white paper entitled `China's Peaceful Development Road` which stated:

China's development will never pose a threat to anyone;....instead it can bring more development opportunities and bigger markets for the rest of the world. It is a serious choice and solemn promise made by the Chinese government and the Chinese people.

Japan, however, described China as a "considerable threat" because of its tendency to secrecy and military build-up. Taro Aso, Japan's foreign minister, told reporters: `The content of China's military expenditure is difficult for outsiders to know, and that fuels suspicion.` [12] In 2006 China ranked ` as the world's sixth largest economy after the U.S. Japan, Germany, Britain and France.......China's GDP was expected to reach $2.16 trillion in 2005.` In 2004 ` China devoured 7.4% of the world's crude oil, 31% of coal, 30% of iron ore, 27% of rolled steel, 25% of alumina and 40% of cement.` [13] China's economy is not invulnerable. The period 2004 to 2006 saw the growth of speculative investment bubbles, particularly in property. If these collapsed there would be a significant increase in the burden on state banks, which are already burdened by bad debts. Also `.....only a relatively small layer of capitalists and the middle class has benefited from China's frenzied and chaotic economic development.` [14] This has generated social inequalities, particularly in the countryside, where there are mounting demonstrations over corrupt officials, taxes, unchecked property development on farmers land, poor wages, etc.

China plays a key part in the world economy. Its demand for raw materials helps support the economies of Japan, S. Korea, South-east Asia and Australia. China, with Japanese and other Asian central banks finances about 80% to 90%, of the huge U.S. deficit. The credit crunch crisis of 2007-2009 in the U.S. will put that country at an increased risk of being vulnerable to being in debt to Chinese financial interests. China has $875 billion in foreign currency reserves, the greatest amount on Earth and these reserves grew by $20 billion a month in 2008.

The fear is that China is playing a long game, gradually sapping the strength of the U.S. economy by flooding the market with cheap goods. The scene is set for a period of tension between the current top dog and its east Asian rival... [15]

Hundreds of years worth of inter-action between the West and China, has left the Chinese seeming still strange and dangerous, hence imagery of Chinese aggressiveness in children's comics, for example : The Chinese were to be exploited economically, hence the need to portray them as absurd and incapable of looking after themselves. Socially the Chinese were likened by elements of Western media as being ungrateful towards their superiors. There always seemed to be a need in British society, to demonise or create a scapegoat of a disadvantaged group within that society; who are deemed to be a threat. In roughly the first twenty five years of the twentieth century, it was the Chinese despite the fact that Chinese people in the West were beginning to make a significant contribution to their adopted homelands in professional jobs. Economically the fate of Chinese labour in the West was tied up partially with capitalism and its need for cheap labour. The reputation within Britain, for example, for Chinese people to be hardworking, added to their attractiveness as labourers. Political reasons behind the mainly negative portrayal of the Chinese in Western comics, magazines and newspapers included the sheer political power of the West over China and persecution of the weakest. Economic and social reasons behind the portrayal in the above mentioned media (e.g. children's comics, magazines and newspapers) included this weakness and "otherness/strangeness" which hundreds of years of inter-action, between China and the West had not changed. By the first decade of the twentieth century Chinese were still being portrayed as dangerous and aggressive in the popular media. The Chinese were to be exploited economically; hence the need to portray them as absurd and incapable of looking after themselves. Socially, their alleged ingratitude, as well as the other characteristics associated with the word "yellow" were connected with them. In the first twenty five years of the twentieth century it was the powerless Chinese who were looked down upon. Today, loosely speaking, it is gypsies or travellers who have taken the place of the Chinese.

The successful 2008 Olympics in Beijing showed the world that China could stand tall amidst the nations of the globe and shake off any lingering doubts that it was capable of completing such an onerous task, in that this was an expensive venture. Any serious slip-up in presenting the Olympics would have cost China dearly as far as its reputation is concerned. The Olympics represented another peak in the inconsistent track record of China's history of relationships with the West. Despite the success of the Olympics from the perspective of, not only the Chinese, but the rest of the world, the global economic crisis at the time still loomed large in the minds of politicians, economists and social commentators. By the autumn of 2008, to put it simply, the situation was this :`As we in the West stop spending, the only way to avoid a global recession is for the Chinese, especially, to spend more.` [16]

NOTES

Chapter One
Introduction

[1] The Times January 7th 1905
[2] A.D. Brear 'That Singular People.' Nineteenth-century attitudes to China and Chinese culture, with particular reference to Great Britain. (Thesis submitted to the University of Lancaster for degree of Master of Philosophy April 1981.) p.15

Chapter Two
China's relationship with
The West 1600-1900

[1] K.M.Panikkar, Asia and Western Dominanace (London: George Allen & Unwin,1959),p.144
[2] L.K. Young, British Policy in China 1895-1902 (London: Oxford University Press,1970), p.43
[3] R.Temple, The Genius of China (London: Prion, 1991) p. 60
[4] R.Temple Ibid p.30
[5] R.Temple Ibid p.34
[6] R.Temple Ibid p.99
[7] M.Dillon, Dictionary of Chinese History (London: Frank Cass,1979),p.135

[8] T.Lambert China Insight China: The Big Picture (Sevenoaks:OMF International January-February 2008),p4
[9] T.Lambert Ibid p.4
[10] L.J. Gallagher, China in the Sixteenth Century: The Journals of Matthew Ricci: 1583-1610 (New York, 1953), in C.Mackerras, Western Images of China (Hong Kong: Oxford University Press,1989), p.33
[11] R.Stephenson, "Aspects of Chinese Astronomy" (paper presented at conference on Science and Civilisation in China at the University of Oxford Department for Continuing Education, 23 November 1996)
[12] P.Craddock, " Scientific Techniques and Industrial Processes in Imperial China" (paper presented at conference on Science and Civilisation in China at University of Oxford Department for Continuing Education, 23 November 1996)
[13] R.K. Batchelor, "Shen Fuzong [Michael Alphonsus] (c.1658-1691] traveler and convert to Christianity. Oxford Dictionary of National Biography" [article online] available from http://www.oxforddnb.com/view/printable/95020 Internet; accessed 16 April 2008
[14] R.K. Batchelor Ibid p.2-3
[15] Anon. Obituary,with Anecdotes, of remarkable Persons. The Gentleman`s Magazine August 1805 p779
[16] C.Mackerras op cit p.35
[17] The Guardian 10th December 2005
[18] K.M.Panikkar op cit p.64
[19] G.B.Endacott, A History of Hong Kong (Hong Kong: Oxford University Press,1973),p.14
[20] Rev J.Goldsmith, A Grammar of General Geography for the use of schools and Young Persons (London: Longman et al,c.1824) pp 49-50
[21] J.Pope-Hennessy,Verandah Some Episodes In The Crown Colonies 1867-1889 (London: Century Publishing,1984),pp218-219
[22] S.W.Muirhead Crisis Banking In The East The History of the Chartered Mercantile Bank of India, London and China 1853-93 (Aldershot: Scolar Press,1996),p.199
[23] W. Muirhead China and the Gospel (London: James Nisbet,1870),p.66
[24] A.Waley The Opium War Through Chinese Eyes (London: George Allen and Unwin,1960)p154
[25] A.Waley Ibid p.119
[26] A.Waley Ibid p.185
[27] P.Hattaway China`s Christian Martyrs (Oxford : Monarch Books,2007),p.74
[28] P.Hattaway Ibid p.77
[29] The Manchester Guardian 23 November 1842 in J.Gittings," Hong Kong 1842-1997 Opium dreams, new destinies." The Guardian 26 June 1997,p.15
[30] J.Gittings Ibid p.15
[31] L.K. Young British Policy in China 1895-1902 (London: Oxford University Press,1970) p.102
[32] P.Hattaway op cit p.65
[33] B.B.C. Radio 4 *Reith Lectures 2008 Chinese Vistas* " English Lessons" Episode 2 May 14th 2008
[34] The Times December 26th 1869 in A.D. Brear op cit p.27
[35] The Illustrated London News April 13th 1861 in A.D. Braer op cit p.26
[36] S Han The Morning Deluge Mao Tsetung and the Chinese Revolution Volume One 1893-1935 (St Albans: Panther Books,1976) ,p.50
[37] E.H.Parker,China`s Intercourse with Europe (Shanghai: Kelly and Walsh Ltd,1890),pp54-55
[38] A.Waley op cit p.33
[39] "China Jim", `Looting at the Summer Palace` Pall Mall Magazine (February 1895),p.274
[40] E.J. Eitel, Europe in China (Hong Kong: Kelly and Walsh Ltd, 1895) p.311
[41] J.Bowring ,Letter from John Bowring to Edgar Bowring March 26th 1849. In archives at John Rylands University Library Manchester. Ref: 1228 R109 210
[42] D.Hurd, `Sir John Bowring The Radical Governor` History Today (October 1967), p.659

[43] Author unknown The London Journal (c.1856 or 1857),p.184
[44] J.Pope-Hennessy op-cit p.196
[45] A Wright ed, Twentieth Century Impressions of Hong Kong, Shanghai and Other Treaty Ports of China (London: Lloyd's Greater Britain Publishing Co,1908) ,p.84
[46] K.Lowe and E.McLaughlin `Sir John Pope-Hennessy and the Native Race Craze`: Colonial Government in Hong Kong,1877-1882` Journal of Imperial and Commonwealth History (May 1992),p.225
[47] P.Ziegler, King Edward VIII The Official Biography (London: Fontana,1991),p.145

Chapter Three
The Nemesis of China's Isolation:
The Boxer Uprising

[1] Dowling. "Mr Dowling's Electronic Passport, Chinese HistoryThe Boxer Rebellion"[article on-line] available from http://www.mrdowling.com/613-boxer.html; Internet; accessed 15 April 2008.
[2] Capt.F.E. Younghusband `A Plea for the Control of China` The National Review (October 1900), pp.214-5
[3] "Ignotus " `The Coming Storm In The Far East` The National Review (December 1899), p.502
[4] "Ignotus" Ibid p.496
[5] L.K. Young British Policy in China 1895-1902 (London: Oxford University Press,1970) p.168
[6] Anon `The Break-Up of China, and Our Interest in It` The Atlantic Monthly (August 1899),p.277
[7] L.K. Young op cit p.19
[8] Anon op cit p.277
[9] L.K. Young op cit p.118
[10] From an unpublished account of the Boxer War by Admiral Sir William Creswell, then commanding the Queensland naval contingent (private collection) p.5
[11] P.F Mattheisen,A.C.Young and P.Coustillas eds Collected Letters of George Gissing Volume 8 (Athens,Ohio: Ohio University Press,1996),p.69

Chapter Four
Orientalist Theories and
British Imperialism in China

[1] E.Said Orientalism Western Conceptions of the Orient (Harmondsworth: Penguin Books,1995),p.23
[2] J.Mackenzie, Orientalism. History,Theory and the Arts (Manchester: Manchester University Press,1996),p.14
[3] L.Newton Hayes `The Most Helpful Books on China` The Chinese Recorder (May 1925) ,p.300
[4] S.W. Williams The Middle Kingdom, A Survey of the Geography, Government, Education, Social Life, Arts ,Religion, etc of the Chinese Empire and Its Inhabitants Vol 2 (New York: John Wiley,1851) pp95-99 in C.Mackerras op.cit p.49
[5] Author unknown. Household Words (August 22 1857),p.184
[6] C.Mackerras op cit p.44

[7] Author unknown `Are missionaries in any way responsible for the present disturbances in China? The Chinese Recorder (December 1900), p.613
[8] A.R.Colquhoun. China in Transformation (London: Harper and Brothers,1912),p.15

Chapter Five
The Yellow Peril
The Chinese As a threat

[1] Wikipedia contributors `Yellow Peril` *Wikipedia The Free Encyclopaedia* 18 March 2008 04:23 UTC< http://en.wikipedia.org/w/index.php?title=Yellow_Peril&oldid=199019635>
[2] Anon. The Oxford Dictionary of Quotations (Oxford: Oxford University Press, 1977,2nd ed),p.238
[3] C.Blake," Chinese Vice In England. A view of terrible conditions at Close Range" The Sunday Chronicle,2 December 1906,p.1
[4] C.Blake 9 December 1906 p.2
[5] BBC Radio 4 *Chinese in Britain* "Steam and Starch" May 3rd 2007.
[6] Western Mail July 12th 1911
[7] Ibid July 12th 1911
[8] Ibid July 13th 1911
[9] Ibid July 13th 1911 ?
[10] Ibid July 21st 1911
[11] Ibid July 22nd 1911
[12] The Cardiff Citizen July 22nd 1911
[13] Western Mail July 24th 1911
[14] J.M.Cayford `In Search of John Chinaman`: Press Representations of The Chinese in Cardiff 1906-1911` Llafur 5(4) 1991 p.39
[15] J.M.Cayford Ibid p.40
[16] J.M.Cayford Ibid p.42
[17] J.M.Cayford Ibid p.45
[18] J.M.Cayford Ibid p.47
[19] J.M.Cayford Ibid p.48
[20] The Liverpool Chinatown Business Association"The History of Chinatown" [article on-line] available from http://web.ukonline.co.uk/lcba/ba/history.html; Internet; accessed 16 April 2008
[21] M.L. Wong Chinese Liverpudlians(Liverpool: The Liver Press, 1989), p.6
[22] M.L.Wong Ibid p.19
[23] C. Holmes ed. Immigrants and Minorities in British Society (London: George Allen and Unwin,1978), p.115
[24] BBC Radio 4's *Chinese in Britain* "From Ship to Shore" Episode 3` May 2nd 2007
[25] C.Holmes op cit p.70
[26] H.Scheffauer `The Chinese in England ` The London Magazine (June 1911),p.465
[27] H.Scheffauer `The Chinese in England Part Two ` The London Magazine (July 1911) p.645
[28] W.T.Power Recollections of a three year residence in China (London: Richard Bentley,1853),p.103
[29] W.T. Power Ibid p.202
[30] J.D.`Ewes China,Australia and the Pacific Islands, in the years 1855-56 (London: Richard Bentley, 1857),p.278
[31] H.Knollys English Life In China (London: Smith,Elder,1885), p.142
[32] The Times August 13th 1878

[33] P.Richardson 'The Recruiting of Chinese Indentured Labour For The South African Gold-Mines,1903-1908 Journal of African History (vol 18(1) 1977) ,p.86
[34] B.L.Putnam Weale The Reshaping of The Far East Volume 1 (London: Macmillan and Co,Ltd,1905), p.90
[35] M.T.Bryson The Land of The Pigtail (London: Sunday School Union,1905),pp1-2
[36] J.Spence The China Helpers.Western advisers in China 1620-1960 (London: The Bodley Head,1969), p.44
[37] A.Conan Doyle The Adventures of Sherlock Holmes (London: Longman Group Ltd,1979),p.125
[38] J.London The Valley of the Moon (London: Mills and Boon Ltd,1914)p.424
[39] Boy's Friend May 16th 1925 p.723
[40] Boy's Leader June 10th 1905 p.216
[41] B.B.C. Radio Four Reith Lecture 2008: *Chinese Vistas "English Lessons"* Episode 2 May 14th 2008
[42] Edinburgh Review 1805. Exact Date Unknown
[43] Victoria and Albert Museum Penny Dreadfuls and Comics.English Periodicals for children from Victorian Times to the Present Day (London: Victoria and Albert Museum,1983),p.22
[44] Wikipedia contributors,'Yellow Peril' *Wikipedia, The Free Encyclopedia*, 11 July 2008, 12:58 UTC, http://en.wikipedia.org/w/index.php?title=Yellow_Peril&oldid=225008603[accessed 23 July 2008]
[45] South China Morning Post(Hong Kong) August 27th 1908
[46] South China Morning Post(Hong Kong) March 3rd 1908
[47] L.K. Young British Policy in China 1895-1902 (London: Oxford University Press,1970),pp86-87
[48] J.Ch'en China and the West (London: Hutchinson,1979),pp57-58
[49] J.Seed " Untold London The Chinese in Limehouse 1900-1940" http://www.untoldlondon.org.uk/archives/TRA43336.html; Internet; accessed April 16 2008
[50] G.A. Wade 'The Cockney John Chinaman.' English Illustrated Magazine (July 1900),p.304
[51] G.A. Wade Ibid p.307
[52] Wikipedia contributors, 'Yellow Peril', *Wikipedia, The Free Encyclopedia*, 11 July 2008,12:58 UTC, <http://en.wikipedia.org/wiki/Yellow_Peril&oldid=225008603>[accessed July 23 2008]
[53] J.Seed op cit
[54] J.Seed op cit
[55] J.Seed op cit
[56] J.Seed op cit
[57] J.Seed op cit
[58] J.Seed op cit
[59] J.Seed op cit
[60] J.Seed op cit
[61] J.Seed op cit
[62] J.Seed op cit
[63] J.Seed op cit
[64] J.O.P. Bland 'The Yellow Peril' The Nineteenth Century and After (May 1912), p.1028
[65] A Member of the Whip Club. Dictionary of the Vulgar Tongue (London: Printed for C.Chappel,1811), no page number.
[66] S. Moore 'Tales from The Yellow Emporium Oriental Forteana. The Hairy Boy of China' Fortean Times 30 (c.early 1980s) p.45
[67] S.Moore 'Tales from The Yellow Emporium Oriental Forteana. Hairy Dilemma' Fortean Times 33 (Autumn 1980) p.41
[68] Wikipedia contributors,'Yellow Peril' , Wikipedia The Free Encyclopedia,19 June 2007,15:08 UTC, http://en.Wikipedia.org/w/index.php?title=Yellow_Peril&oldid=139213516 [accessed 29 June 2007]
[69] F.Scott Fitzgerald The Great Gatsby (Harmondsworth: Penguin,1990),p.18
[70] C.Bolt Victorian attitudes to race (London: Routledge & Kegan Paul,1971), p.200

Chapter Six
The Yellow Peril scare in the United States of America

[1] S.C. Miller "The Unwelcome Immigrant: The American Image of the Chinese, 1785-1882 " in "The Yellow Peril : Anti-Asian Sentiment in 19th and early 20th Century America." [article on-line] available from http://www.erasofelegance.com/asianhistory.html ; Internet; accessed 16 April 2008
[2] B.B.C. Radio 4 *Reith Lectures 2008: Chinese Vistas* " English Lessons" May 14th 2008.
[3] Anon. Immigration The Journey To America. The Chinese. [article on-line] available from http://library.thinkquest.org/20619/Chinese.html; Internet; accessed 22 August 2008
[4] S.C.Miller op cit
[5] M.A. Jones Destination America (London: Book Club Associates, 1976), p227
[6] J.C.Mohr Plague and Fire Battling Black Death And The 1900 Burning Of Honolulu`s China Town (New York: Oxford University Press,2005),p.57
[7] W.Chow Letter to Editor January 23 1900 in Pacific Commercial Advertiser (Honolulu) January 25 1900 p.3 in J.C.Mohr Ibid p.149
[8] S.Winchester A Crack In the Edge of the World (London: Penguin,2006),p.316
[9] J.London The Valley of the Moon (London: Mills and Boon Ltd,1914),pp421-422
[10] J.London Ibid p.422
[11] J.London Ibid p.425
[12] Wikipedia contributors, `Yellow Peril` *Wikipedia, The Free Encyclopedia*, 11 July 2008, 12:58 UTC, <http://en.wikipedia.org/w/index.php?title=Yellow_Peril&oldid=225008603[accessed 23 July 2008]
[13] The Guardian 10 December 2005,pp25-26
[14] Wikipedia contributors, ` Yellow Peril` op cit.

Chapter Seven
Chinese Indentured Labour
In South Africa

[1] Public Record Office (PRO) CO 291vol. 51,no. 38975/02 , Original correspondence, Perry- Secretary of State, 1902 in K. L Harris `Rand Capitalists and Chinese Resistance` Contree 35 (1994) p.19
[2] P.C. Campbell, Chinese coolie emigration to countries within the British Empire New York 1923 pp45,56; H.F. MacNair,The Chinese abroad: Their position and protection, a study in international law and relations, Shangai(sic) 1925 pp62-63;L.Mitchison, The overseas Chinese, London 1961 p21; P. Snow, The star raft: Chinese encounter with Africa New York 1987 pp45-46 in K. L. Harris ibid p19
[3] Ta Chen Chinese migrations with special reference to labour conditions Washington DC 1923 p.129; L Pan Sons of the Yellow Emperor: The story of the overseas Chinese, London 1990 pp63-64 in K.L. Harris ibid p.19
[4] K.L. Harris Ibid p.19
[5] H.M.Lai The United States in L.Pan (ed) The Encyclopedia of the Chinese Overseas (London: Taylor and Francis Books Ltd, 1998) pp261-262; K.L.Harris `South Africa` in L.Pan (ed) Ibid pp360-361 in K. L.Harris "Not a Chinaman`s Chance" : Chinese labour in South Africa and the United States of America

Historia 52(2) November 2006 p181
[6] The New York Times May 17th 1903 [article on-line] available from http://query.nytimes.com/mem/archive-free/pdf?_r=18res=9AOOEED71F3OE733A25754CIA9639C946297D6CF&oref=slogin; Internet; accessed April 22 2008
[7] K.L.Harris A History of the Chinese in South Africa to 1912 PhD Thesis University of South Africa, Pretoria, 1998 pp 137-142 in K.L Harris " Not a Chinaman's Chance": Chinese labour in South Africa and the United States of America Historia 52(2) November 2006 p184
[8] National Archives .`Schedule` FO2/899 9(1) P.36.
[9] L. Pan Sons of the Yellow Emperor: The story of the overseas Chinese(London: 1990) p.26 in K.L. Harris Ibid p.188
[10] L. Pan Ibid p.277 in K.L.Harris Ibid p.188
[11] K.L.Harris Ibid p.192
[12] Email from K.L.Harris 20th November 2007. Department of Historical and Heritage Studies. University of Pretoria. South Africa
[13] P.Richardson Chinese Mine Labour in The Transvaal (London and Basingstoke:The Macmillan Press Ltd, 1982) p166 in K.L Harris The Chinese in South Africa: a preliminary overview to 1910 Kleio 26 1994 p.23
[14] Indian Opinion 27 April 1907, 18 May 1907 in K.L.Harris Ibid p25
[15] Email from K.L.Harris 16th August 2008.

Chapter Eight
The Red Peril:
The British and The Rise of Communism in China

1 G.F. Hudson Fifty Years of Communism Theory and Practice 1917-1967 (Harmondsworth: Pelican,1971),p.124
[2] Letter from Dr Robert Bickers 29th May 1997. Faculty of Oriental Studies, University of Cambridge.
[3] Undated in J.Ch`en op.cit p.51
[4] J.Ch`en op.cit pp 51-52
[5] W.G.Sewell MS 16/File 19 Unpublished novel p.65 Archives as found at School of Oriental and African Studies, London.
[6] W.G. Sewell Ibid p.98
[7] P.Gillingham At The Peak Hong Kong Between The Wars (Hong Kong:Macmillan Publishers Limited,1983),p.43
[8] P.Gillingham Ibid p.43
[9] Overland China Mail July 30th 1925
[10] V.Kit-yiu Ho Hong Kong Government`s Attitude to the Canton-Hong Kong Strike and Boycott of 1925-1926(Master of Studies Thesis: University of Oxford,1985),p.6 and p.79
[11] V.Kit-yiu Ho Ibid p.6 and p.79
[12] The South China Morning Post May 27th 1925
[13] The South China Morning Post Ibid May 27th 1925
[14] J.Downes The Island Of Paradise. Chupacabra, UFO Crash Retrievals and Accelerated Evolution on The Island of Puerto Rico (Bidiford: CFZ Press, 2008), pp 191-2.

[15] M.Hogan et al Kowloon Disturbances 1966 Report of Commission of Inquiry (Hong Kong: Government Press,1966),p.148.

Chapter Nine
Conclusion

[1] The Times December 20th 2004
[2] The Guardian December 12th 2004
[3] The Guardian March 6th 2007
[4] The Guardian February 5th 2007
[5] London Review of Books July 5th 2007
[6] The Guardian February 8th 2007
[7] London Review of Books op cit
[8] London Review of Books op cit
[9] The New York Times August 18th 2007
[10] BBC Radio 4's *Reith Lecture 2008 Chinese Vistas* " English Lessons" Episode 2 May 14th 2008.
[11] The Guardian November 23rd 2005
[12] The Guardian December 23rd 2005
[13] John Chan " Market commentators cheer China's revised economic figures"[article on-line] available from http://www.wsws.org/articles/2006/jan2006/chin-j03prn.shtml; Internet; accessed 16 April 2008
[14] J.Chan Ibid p.2
[15] The Guardian March 6th 2006
[16] The Guardian October 15th 2008

BIBLIOGRAPHY

Primary Sources.

Public Archives.

John Rylands University Library, Manchester.
        John Bowring Papers.
Rhodes House Library, Oxford.
        Lugard Papers.
        Nathan Papers.
School of Oriental and African Studies Library Archives,London.
        Sir F.Maze Papers
Methodist Missionary Society Archives.
        Sewell Papers.

British Newspapers, *National.*

Sunday Chronicle: December 2nd 1906,December 9th 1906
The Guardian: June 26th 1997, December 12th 2004, November 23rd 2005,December 10th 2005,December 23rd 2005, March 6th 2006,February 8th 2007,March 6th 2007,October 15th 2008.
The Times: May 16th 1901, October 10th 1903, May 12th 1904, July 11th 1904, January 7th 1905, January 12th 1905, May 28th -29th 1907, July 9th 1925, August 27th 1925, December 20th 2004.

British Newspapers, *Provincial.*

The Cardiff Citizen: July 22nd 1911.
Western Mail: July 12th 1911, July 13th 1911, July 21st 1911, July 22nd 1911, July 24th 1911.

British Magazines and Periodicals

Fortean Times: Number 30. Early 1980s. Number 33. Autumn 1980.
The Illustrated London News: July 1900.
London Review of Books. July 5th 2007.
Penny Pictorial Magazine: An issue within vol.1-2 1899, issue for week ending March 17th 1900, issue for week ending April 14th 1900.
Punch: July 25th 1900

British Comics.

Boys Best Story Paper: November 23rd 1911, February 1st 1912, June 8th 1912.
Boys Friend: Issue for week ending May 16th 1925, issue for week ending May 30th 1925.
Boys Leader: Issue for week ending April 16th 1904, issue for week ending June 10th 1905.
Girls Friend Library: May 1st 1925

Hong Kong Newspapers

Hong Kong Daily Press: October 1st 1884, October 6th 1884.
Hong Kong Telegraph: May 2nd 1900, May 26th 1900, July 2nd 1900, August 4th 1900.
Overland China Mail: August 4th 1900, February 21st 1905, April 8th 1905, April 22nd 1905, August 31st 1912, June 18th 1925, July 23rd 1925, July 30th 1925, August 6th 1925.
South China Morning Post: March 3rd 1908, August 27th 1908, April 18th 1925, May 25th, 26th, 27th 1925, June 5th 1925, September 3rd 1925, September 8th 1925, October 3rd 1925, October 9th 1925, March 4th 1933, May 5th 1967.

Shanghai Newspaper.

Shanghai Mercury Emergency Edition: June 20th 1925, June 27th 1925.

Secondary Sources.

Anon (August 1899), *The Break-Up of China, and Our Interest in It* in *The Atlantic Monthly*.

Anon, (June 28th 1997), *How Hong Kong can change China*. in *The Economist*.
Anon, (August 1805) Obituary, with Anecdotes, of remarkable Persons in *The Gentleman's Magazine*.
Author unknown, (December 1900), Are missionaries in any way responsible for the present disturbances in China? in *The Chinese Recorder*.
Author unknown, (1900), China of To-day. *The Yellow Peril*. George Newnes Ltd.
Author unknown, (1805), *Edinburgh Review*.
Author unknown, (August 22 1857), *Household Words*.
Author unknown, (1856 or 1857), *The London Journal*.
Dr H.Baker, (1979), Ancestral Images. A Hong Kong Album. *South China Morning Post*.
J.Dyer Ball, (1926), *Things Chinese* J.Murray.
W.G Beasley, (1971), *The Modern History of Japan*. Weidenfeld and Nicholson.
L. Bianco, (1972), *Origins of the Chinese Revolution* 1915-1949. Oxford University Press.
Dr R.Bickers, (May 29 1997), Private letter.
C.Blake, (December 2 and 9 1906), *Chinese vice in England. A view of terrible conditions at Close Range* in *The Sunday Chronicle*.
J.O.P. Bland, (May 1912) , *The Yellow Peril in The Nineteenth Century and After*.
C.Bolt, (1971), Victorian attitudes to Race. Routledge & Kegan Paul.
G.Bovill, (1976), *Knight or Knave? A Soldier of Fortune in China*. Privately published.
A.D.Brear(1981), `That Singular People` Nineteenth – century attitudes to China and Chinese culture, with particular reference to Great Britain. Master of Philosophy thesis University of Lancaster.
M.T. Bryson,(1905), The Land of the Pigtail. Sunday School Union.
J.M. Cayford, (vol 5 part 4 1991), *In Search of John Chinaman: Press Representations of The Chinese in Cardiff 1906-1911 in Llafur*.
Chan Lau Kit-ching, (1990), *China, Britain and Hong Kong, 1895-1945*. Chinese University Press.
J.Ch`en, (1979), *China and the West*. Hutchinson.
J.Ch`en, (1967), *Mao and the Chinese Revolution*. Oxford University Press.
China Association, (1900), Annual Report 1900. Gazette Printing Office.
I.F.Clarke,(1978), *Tale of the Future*. The Library Association.
J.Clegg, (1994), *Fu Manchu and the Yellow Peril*. Trentham Books.
N.R.Clifford,(1991), *Spoilt Children of Empire. Westerners in Shanghai and the Chinese Revolution of the 1920s*. University Press of New England.
A.R. Colquhoun, (1912), *China in Transformation*. Harper & Brothers.
A.R Colquhoun, (1908), *Dan to Beersheba*. William Heinemann.
A.R. Colquhoun, (1900), *The Overland to China*. Harper & Brothers.
Committee of Hong Kong-Kowloon Chinese Compatriots of All Circles for the Struggle Against Persecution by the British Authorities in Hong Kong, eds,(1967), The May Upheaval in Hong Kong.
A.Conan Doyle, (1979), *The Adventures of Sherlock Holmes*. Longman Group Ltd.
S.Couling, (1917), *Encyclopaedia Sinica*. Kelly & Walsh Ltd.
P.Coustillas, P.F. Mattheisen and A.C.Young eds,(1996), *Collected Letters of George Gissing Volume 8*. Ohio University Press.
Sir A.Creswell, (1900), *Unpublished account of the Boxer War*. Private collection.
M.P.Curtis and B.E.Eaden,eds,(1978), *Non-Current Serials A Select List of Holdings in the University Library*. Cambridge University Library.
M.Dillon, (1979), *Dictionary of Chinese History*. Frank Cass.
J.Dimbleby, (1997), *The Last Governor.Chris Patten and the Handover of Hong Kong*. Little,Brown and Company.
A.Diosy, (1905), *The New Far East*. Cassel & Co Ltd.
J. Downes, (2008), *The Island of Paradise*. Centre for Fortean Zoology Press.
Sir A. Conan Doyle, (1979), The Adventures of Sherlock Holmes. Longman Group Ltd.

N.P. Edwards,(1900), *The Story of China with a description of events relating to the present struggle.* Hutchinson & Co.
E.J Eitel, (1895), *Europe in China.* Kelly & Walsh Ltd.
Encyclopaedia Britannica Volume 5, (1969), William Benton.
G.B. Endacott,(1973), *A History of Hong Kong.* Oxford University Press.
J.K. Fairbank,(1979), *The United States and China.* Harvard University Press.
H.A. Giles, (1878), *A Glossary of Reference on Subjects Connected with the Far East.* Messrs. Lane, Crawford & Co.
H.A. Giles, (1882), *Historic China.* Thomas De La Rue & Co.
H.A. Giles, translator, (1880), *Strange Stories from a Chinese Studio.* Thomas De La Rue & Co.
Rev. J.Goldsmith,(c.1824), *A Grammar of General Geography for the use of schools and Young Persons.* Longman et al.
J.Gittings, (April 12 1997), The real China story in *The Guardian.*
J. Gittings, (June 26 1997), Hong Kong 1842-1997 Opium dreams, new destinies in *The Guardian.*
J.Goody, (1996), *The East in the West.* Cambridge University Press.
D.W.S. Gray and K.L.Pratt,(1973), *China An Index to European Visual and Aural Material.* Crosby Lockwood Staples.
M.E.Hammond with E.Saenger and J.D.Stewart, eds, (1955), *British Union Catalogue of Periodicals Volume One A-C.* Butterworth Scientific Publications.
S.Han, (1976), *The Morning Deluge. Mao Tsetung and the Chinese Revolution Volume One 1893-1935.* Panther Books.
Hansard - House of Commons, (2 August 1900), Wyman and Sons Ltd.
Hansard - House of Commons, (27 September 1949), H.M.S.O
K.L.Harris, (vol 52 part 2 November 2006), Not a Chinaman's Chance: Chinese Labour in South Africa and the United States of America in *Historia.*
K.L.Harris, (vol 26 1994), The Chinese in South Africa: a preliminary overview to 1910 in *Kleio.*
K.L.Harris, (vol 35 1994), Rand Capitalists and Chinese Resistance in *Contree.*
P.Hattaway, (2007), *China's Christian Martyrs.* Monarch Books.
B.C. Henry, (1886), *Ling-Nam or Interior Views of Southern China .* S.W Partridge and Co.
V. Kit-yiu Ho, (1985), *Hong Kong Governments Attitude to the Canton-Hong Kong Strike and Boycott of 1925-1926.* Master of Studies thesis, University of Oxford.
E.J. Hobsbawm, (1972), *Bandits.* Pelican Books.
C.Holmes,ed, (1978), *Immigrants and Minorities in British Society.* George Allen & Unwin.
B.Hornadge, (1976), *The Yellow Peril. A Squint at some Australian attitudes towards Orientals.* Review Publications Pty. Ltd.
G.F.Hudson, (1971), *Fifty Years of Communism Theory and Practice 1917-1967.* Pelican.
D.Hurd, (October 1967), Sir John Bowring The Radical Governor. in *History Today.*
Ignotus, (December 1899), The Coming Storm In The Far East. in *The National Review.*
'J.C'(1845), Part of A Letter from Hong Kong descriptive of that Colony. Smith, Elder & Co.
M.B. Jensen, (August 1951), Opportunists in South China During the Boxer Rebellion. in *Pacific Historical Review.*
M.A.Jones, (1976), *Destination America.* Book Club Associates.
F-T Jung, (1993), *Hong Kong In Chinese History.* Columbia University Press.
M.Kajima, (1978), *The Diplomacy of Japan 1894-1922 Volume 2. Anglo-Japanese Alliance and Russo-Japanese War.* Kajima Institute of International Peace.
P.H.B. Kent, (1937), *The Twentieth Century in the Far East.* Edward Arnold & Co.
V.G. Kiernan, (1988), *The Lords of Human Kind.* The Cresset Library.
T.Lambert, (Jan-Feb 2008), *China: The Big Picture* in *China Insight.* OMF International.
J.London, (1914), *The Valley of the Moon.* Mills and Boon Ltd.
K.Lowe and E.McLaughlin, (May 1992), *Sir John Pope Hennessy and the 'Native Race Craze': Colo-*

nial Government in Hong Kong, 1877-1882. in Journal of Imperial and Commonwealth History.
P.Lowe, (1981), *Britain in the Far East:a survey from 1819 to the present.* Longman.
J.Mackenzie, (1996), *Orientalism.History,Theory and the Arts.* Manchester University Press.
C.Mackerras, (1989), *Western Images of China.* Oxford University Press.
J.S.Major, (Spring 1986), *Asia Through a Glass Darkly: Stereotypes of Asians in Western Literature in Asia Society's Focus on Asia Studies Contemporary Literature.*
N.Matthews, M.Doreen Wainwright, ed.by J.D.Pearson,(1977), *A Guide To Manuscripts and Documents in the British Isles Relating to the Far East.* Oxford University Press.
A.Mee,(no date), *I See All.* Amalgamated Press.
N.Miners,(1987), *Hong Kong under Imperial Rule 1912-1941.* Oxford University Press.
J.C.Mohr,(2005), *Plague and Fire Battling Black Death And The 1900 Burning of Honolulu's China Town.* Oxford University Press.
S.Moore, (c.1980s), Tales from the Yellow Emporium - Oriental Forteana. The Hairy Boy of China in *Fortean Times* #30
S.Moore, (c.1980s), Tales from the Yellow Emporium - Oriental Forteana. *Hairy Dilemma* in *Fortean Times.* #33
G.Mosely, (1968), *China, Empire to People's Republic.* B.T. Batsford Ltd.
S.W.Muirhead,(1996), *Crisis Banking In The East The History of the Chartered Mercantile Bank of India, London and China* 1853-1893. Scolar Press.
W.Muirhead, (1870), *China and the Gospel.* James Nisbet.
D.Mullen, (1985), *Shanghai Bridge.* Hamlyn Paperbacks.
A.J. Nathan, (1973), *Modern China 1840-1972 An Introduction to Sources and Research Aids.* Centre for Chinese Studies University of Michigan.
L. Newton Hayes, (May 1925), *The Most Helpful Books on China in The Chinese Recorder.*
I.Nish, (1972), *Alliance in Decline.* The Athlone Press.
K.M. Panikkar,(1959), *Asia and Western Dominance.* George Allen & Unwin.
E.H. Parker, (1890), *China's intercourse with Europe.* Kelly & Walsh Ltd.
P.W. Pitcher, (1912), *In and about Amoy.* Methodist Publishing House in China.
J.Pope-Hennessy (1984), *Verandah - Some Episodes In The Crown Colonies 1867-1889.* Century Publishing.
J.T.Pratt, (no date), *China and Britain.* Collins.
V.Purcell, (1974), *The Boxer Uprising - A Background Study.* Archon Books.
B.L.Putnam Weale, (1905), *The Reshaping of The Far East Volume 1.* Macmillan and Co,Ltd.
K.W.Rea ed, (1977), *The Collected Papers of Earl Swisher 1925-1926.* Westview Press,Inc.
P.Richardson,(1982), *Chinese Mine Labour in The Transvaal.* The Macmillan Press Ltd.
P.Richardson,(vol 18 no 1 1977), *The Recruiting of Chinese Indentured Labour For The South African Gold-Mines 1903-1908* in *Journal of African History.*
R.W. Rigby, (1980), *The May 30th Movement - Events and Themes.* Dawson.
J.M. Roberts, (1985), *Triumph of the West.* B.B.C.
J.Robottom,(1980), *Modern China.* Longman.
A.Room,(1995), *Brewer's Dictionary of Phrase and Fable.* Cassell Publishers Ltd.
Royal Institute of International Affairs, (1928), Survey of International Affairs 1925. Oxford University Press.
E.Said, (1994), *Culture and Imperialism.* Vintage.
E.Said, (1995), *Orientalism - Western Conceptions of the Orient.* Penguin Books.
H. Scheffauer, (June 1911), *The Chinese in England* in *The London Magazine.*
H.Scheffauer, (July 1911), *The Chinese in England Part Two* in *The London Magazine.*
H.Z. Schiffrin, (1968), *Sun Yat-sen and the Origins of the Chinese Revolution.* University of California Press.
F.Scott Fitzgerald, (1990), *The Great Gatsby.* Penguin.

M.P. Shiel,(1898), *The Yellow Da*nger. Grant Richards.

Y.S.Sun, (1988), Address to the students of Hong Kong University in Renditions 29-30 1988. Chinese University of Hong Kong.
L.L.T`ang, (1928), *The Foundations of Modern China*. Noel Douglas.
J.Hudson Taylor, (1903), *A Retrospect. Morgan and Scott and The China Inland Mission*.
R.Temple, (1991), *The Genius of China*. Prion.
H.Ukhtomski, (February 1902), *The Genius of China* in the *Contemporary Review*.
Victoria and Albert Museum, (1983), *Penny Dreadfuls and Comics. English Periodicals for children from Victorian Times to the Present Day*. Victoria and Albert Museum.
G.A. Wade, (July 1900), *The Cockney John Chinaman* in *English Illustrated Magazine*.
A.Waley, (1960), *The Opium War through Chinese Eyes*. George Allen and Unwin.
P.J.Waller, (September 1985), *Immigration into Britain: The Chinese* in *History Today*.
J.Warner, (1981), *Hong Kong Illustrated News and Views 1840-1890*. John Warner Publications.
B.L. Putnam Weale, (1905), *The Reshaping of the Far East Vol.1* Macmillan and Co,Ltd.
B.Peh T`i Wei, (1987), *Shanghai - Crucible of Modern China*. Oxford University Press.
B.S. White, (1996), *Hong Kong: Somewhere between Heaven and Earth*. Oxford University Press.
E.Wilkinson, (1975), *The history of Imperial China - A Research Guide*. Harvard University Press.
S.Winchester, (2006), *A Crack In* The Edge of The World. Penguin.
M.L.Wong, (1989), Chinese Liverpudlians. Liver Press.
A.Wright,ed (1908), *Twentieth Century Impressions of Hong Kong, Shanghai and Other Treaty Ports of China*. Lloyd`s Greater Britain Publishing Co.
P.Yapp,ed, (1983), *The Travellers Dictionary of Quotations. Who Said What About Where?* Routledge and Kegan Paul.
J.D. Young, (1981 vol.19 pt.2) China`s Role in Two Hong Kong Disturbances: *A Sceanario for the future?* in Journal of Oriental Studies.
L.K. Young, (1970), *British Policy in China 1895-1902*. Oxford University Press.
Capt.F.E.Younghusband,(October 1900), *A Plea for the Control of China* in The National Review.
P.Ziegler, (1991), *King Edward VIII The Official Biography*. Fontana.

ACKNOWLEDGEMENTS

Thanks to the following for their help with this book:

Jon Downes, at CFZ Press, CFZ Communications, ,for publishing this book, Dr Karen Harris, full professor in the Department of Historical and Heritage Studies and director of the archives at the University of Pretoria, South Africa for information on the Chinese in South Africa. Val Hayward for the Chinese statue. Dr Donal Lowry, my tutor at Oxford Brookes University 1996-1999. Nic Moran, PCSOS247, Macclesfield for tireless help with my computer ignorance. Dr John Seed, historian, School of Arts, Roehampton University, London, for information on the Chinese community in Limehouse, London. Peter Rawlins for proof reading. Martin Skirvin for the photo of the Canton Street sign in Macclesfield and staff at the Bodleian Library, Oxford, the British Library, London, the John Rylands University Library Archives Manchester, the Liverpool Central Library, the Macclesfield Central Library, the National Archives, London, the Rhodes House Library, Oxford, the School of Oriental and African Studies Library, London and the Worcester County Record Office.

If I have accidentally left someone out, please accept my apologies.

Thanks to the Bodleian Library,Oxford, for permission to reproduce the following images:

Front cover of *The Boys` Best Story Paper* of November 23rd 1911. Reference number: Per 2533 b.11
Cartoon `The Yellow Peril` in frontispiece of *The New Far East*. By A.Diosy. Ref no: BJL JM.F00115
Cartoon of Chinese person carrying baskets in *The Yellow Peril. A Squint at some Australian attitudes towards Orientals.* By B.Hornadge. Ref no: M90.G02325. Thanks also to Mr B.Hornadge for permission to reproduce this cartoon.
Front cover of *The Yellow Danger*. By M.P.Shiel. Ref no: 254399 e 67

Thanks to Worcester County Record Office for permission to reproduce the cartoon of the Empress Dowager from *The Rattle of November* 1900. Ref no: 705:385 BA 4351

Thanks to Local Studies Library at Cardiff Central Library for permission to reproduce the photograph of the wrecked Chinese laundry,smashed by rioters in Mackintosh Place,Cardiff,July 1911. Image ID: STR019

RICHARD MUIRHEAD
Publications 1996-2009

Cryptozoology

The Flying Snake of Namibia. Centre for Fortean Zoology Yearbook 1996
Giant Squid, Mystery Boar and Pregnant Snake. *Animals & Men* Issue 14 1997
A Collection of Cat Curiosities. *Animals & Men* Issue 16 1998.
With Jon Downes: The Mystery Animals of Hong Kong. *The Anomalist* Issue 6 Spring 1998
Some Strange Snake Stories. Centre for Fortean Zoology Yearbook 1998
Some Chinese Cryptids. *The Cryptozoology Review* vol 3 no 3 Winter-Spring 1999
Some Chinese Cryptids. Part Two. *The Cryptozoology Review* vol 4 no 1 Summer 2000
The Basilisk or Cockatrice. *The Cryptozoology Review* vol 4 no 1 Summer 2000
With Darren Naish: Unusually coloured frogs in Britain. *Animals & Men* Issue 32 2003
Fortean Zoological Aspects of the Rupert the Bear Stories. Centre for Fortean Zoology Yearbook 2003
Fortean Frogs and Toads. *Animals & Men* Issue 44 2008.
Zoological Curiosities from Hardwicke's Science Gossip Part 1 1865-1867. Centre for Fortean Zoology Yearbook 2008
The Tarasque. Centre for Fortean Zoology Yearbook 2009.

Local History

The Macclesfield and Manchester area earthquake of 1777. *Old Macc Magazine* Issue 44 Summer 2008

Meteorology

A snowdrift in Sherborne, Dorset, February 1978. *Journal of Meteorology*. vol 23 no. 234. December 1998
The Fujiwara Effect: An Introduction. *Journal of Meteorology*. vol 25 no 249. May/June 2000
Hong Kong's last severe typhoon of the 20th century: Typhoon York. *Journal of Meteorology*. vol 25 no 253. November 2000
With Jonathan Webb. The severe hailstorm of September 5th 1998 along the London and Surrey border. *Journal of Meteorology*. vol 26 no 257 March 2001
World weather disasters column. *Journal of Meteorology* October 2001- December 2005
With Jonathan Webb. Severe hailstorm over west Cornwall on 25 August 2000. *Weather*. vol 57 no 10. October 2002
A Rare Hurricane in the South Atlantic: Hurricane Catarina, March 2004. *Journal of Meteorology* vol.29 no 294. December 2004
The cold winter of 1962-1963 in Macclesfield *Old Macc Magazine* Issue 33 Summer 2005
The Odd One:Hurricane Vince 8-11 October 2005. *International Journal of Meteorology* vol 33 332. October 2008
Severe Hailstorms in Central England:12 June 2006. *International Journal of Meteorology* vol 33 no 333. November 2008

Natural History

Black squirrels in Britain *British Wildlife* vol 10 no 2 December 1998

Poetry

Struck by the moon. *Challenging stigma* poetry book. 2007
Residential Home. *Majestic Minds* anthology. 2008
Burma after the cyclone. *Forward Press 20th anniversary anthology*. 2008
Canal bridge thirty-seven. *Homage to Cheshire* anthology. 2009

ABOUT THE AUTHOR

Richard Muirhead was born in the Mid-Levels on Hong Kong island on November 5th 1966 . A few years later he moved with his parents and older brother to Mount Kellett, up on The Peak. His early interests included looking after worms and observing tadpoles at his primary school, the Peak School. One of his earliest memories is of stumbling across an emerald and yellow Bamboo snake or White Lipped Pit Viper, *(Trimeresurus albolabris)* killed within twenty minutes by an over zealous watchman.

Richard also reared a fledgling sparrow up to adulthood, when it flew away one day on tiring of human company. At the age of 8 Richard went to boarding schools in Dorset, England and on reaching 18 went to Teesside Polytechnic in Middlesborough where he studied for and later achieved a BA(Hons) in Humanities, whilst attempting to photograph a green puppy in a local home.

Richard's research career really began at the library of the Hong Kong Royal Observatory, now just the Hong Kong Observatory, where he spent happy hours researching various aspects of meteorology. Half way through his first degree Richard experienced a severe mental breakdown, but returned at the age of 20 to Teeside to finish his degree. By this time he was active in left-wing politics, having travelled widely in China in 1983 and 1984.

From 1990-1991 Richard was a student at the Department of Information and Library Studies of the University College of Wales in Aberystwyth. Here he learnt all aspects of librarianship that existed at the time. This was before the internet was in popular use. Richard obtained a post-graduate diploma in librarianship in 1991. He had only one professional library post, at Age Concern's headquarters in London during 1992. After several years trying to find his feet, as a bookseller in Salisbury, a museum custodian in Shaftesbury, Dorset, a grocer in Oxford, a care worker in Inverness and a horticulture student in Cork, Ireland, he eventually found his niche at Oxford Brookes University where from 1996 to 1999 he studied for a MA in Research in the Humanities. Here he specialized in the notion of China as the 'Yellow Peril'. This book is the expansion of the ideas put forward in the dissertation on this subject. All this time Richard was pursuing research into his cryptozoological, Fortean and other interests and having the research published. After another episode of mental illness between 1997 and 1999. Richard moved from Oxford to Macclesfield, Cheshire in 1998 where he lives alone with a barograph, a rain-gauge, slugs which invade his living room, and the occasional passing butterfly.

INDEX

A

Adams, Henry, (U.S. government advisor) 37
Africa, 10,14,70
Age of Exploration, 15
Algeria, 69
America, 51
American Civil War, 55
Amherst,Lord (British diplomat), 17
Amoy,19
Anglo-Japanese Agreement, 1902, 23
Anglo-Japanese Alliance,1921, 23
Angola 69
Anthony, John (Chinese citizen) 16
Anti-Japanese Riots, San Francisco 1907, 27
Arrow, The (ship) 20,22
Astronomy, 8,14-15
Aso,Taro, (Japanese foreign minister) 71
At The Peak:Hong Kong Between The Wars ,65
Australia, 9,27,44,47, 51,71

B

Bakhunin,Mikhail (Russian anarchist) 34
Barry,Cardiff, 39
Beijing Olympics 2008, 64,71 see also Olympics
Bentham, Jeremy, (social reformer) 21
The Big Four, 50
Blake, Sir Henry,(Hong Kong governor) 27,66
Bland J.O.P., (Sinologist) 51
Bodleian Library, Oxford 16
Boer War, 9, 59-60
Bolsheviks,Bolshevism,"Bolshevists", 63-65
Bowring, Sir John,(Hong Kong governer) 8,21-22
Boxer Uprising, 8-9,11,13,23, 25-28, 40,48
Boxers, 9,25-28, 65
Boys` Best Story Paper November 23rd 1911, 44,51
Boy`s Friend, w/e May 16th 1925,43
Boy`s Leader, w/e June 10th 1905,43
Boys` Realm, 44

Brahe,Tycho, (Danish astronomer)14
British Library Newspaper Library, 9
Brookes, Rev S.M,(Christian martyr) 27
Broome,Australia, 47
Bulletin,The 1881, 44
Burma, 15
Burrage E.H(editor) 44

C

California, 39,55-56,
Canton, 9,14,18-22,26-27,42,64-66
Cardiff,38-41,48
Cardiff Citizen, July 22nd 1911, 40
Cast Iron, 14
Ceramics, 14,16
Ch`en,Jerome (author) 64
Ch`ing (Qing) Dynasty, 14,16-17,25,
Chiang Kai-shek (Chinese leader) 65
Ching Ching`s Own, 1888-1893, 44
Chess, 14
China, barbarian, 7,9,14
China, civilised 7,9,14-15,42,
China In Transformation 34
Chinese Bank,42
Chinese Communist Party, 20-21,64
Chinese Exclusion Act 1882, 37, 55
Chinese Language School,42
Chinese Laundry Blues (song),50
Chinese News Weekly,42
The Chinese Recorder December 1900, 34
Chinese Republican Progress Club,42
Chinese Seamen`s Club, 42
Chinese Seamen`s Welfare Centre,41-42
Chinoiserie, 32, 42,
Christians,19,26,27,34
Christie, Agatha,(author) 50
Clementi, Sir Cecil (Hong Kong governor) 65
Coleridge, Samuel Taylor (poet) 7
The Collected Letters of George Gissing, 28,
Colquhoun,A.R. (author) 34
Comics, Boys 9
Comics, Girls 9

Confucius, (Chinese sage)17-18,21
Culture and Imperialism, 8,31,

D

Darwin,Australia, 47
Darwin,Charles, (biologist) 21
De Quincey,Thomas,7,
Delhi,21
Derby, Australia, 47
Dr Who,51
Downes, Jon (author) 66
Du Halde, Jean-Baptiste,(author) 8,16-17
Dulwich, (steamship) 39

E

East Africa, 14
East India Company, 16,18,59
Edinburgh Review,1805 44
Edward VIII, 23
Eitel E.J (author) 18
Empress Dowager,(Chinese ruler) 23,27-28
Enamel, 14,21
English Illustrated Magazine July 1900, 48
Europe,/European 10-18,21,23,26-27,34,37,41,44,48,50,59,64
Europe in China, 18

F

Fing Su,(fictional Chinese character) 50
First World War,50
Foochow, 19
Footbinding,17,43
Foreric,(steamship) 39
Formby,George,(comedian and singer) 50
Fortean Times no.30, 52
Fortean Times, no.33, 52
Foucault,Michel (historian and philosopher) 31
France/French 4,8,13,15,20-

21,23,27,31,34, 47-48,50,65,70
Fu Manchu, (fictional Chinese character) 48,50

G

Gambling Dens,42,
The General History of China, 16
The Genius of China, 14
*The Gentleman's Magazine August 1805,*16
George III ,17
Germans/Germany, 4,9,13,23,27,47-48,50,57,70
Gillingham,Paul (author) 65
Girl's Friend Library, May 1st 1925 43-44
Glass, 14
Gompers,Samuel, (U.S. labour leader) 37
Gospel, 10
Grammar of General Geography for the Use Of Schools and Young Persons, 17
Great Britain, 13,27,66
The Great Gatsby, 52
Great Proletarian Cultural Revolution, 66
The Guardian December 10th 2005, 17
The Guardian February 5th 2007 ,69
*The Guardian February 8th 2007,*70
*The Guardian March 6th 2007,*69
Gypsies, 71

H

Halde, Du, 8,16-17
Han, Suyin (Chinese author) 21
Harris, Dr Karen,(South African academic) 9
Hawaii, 56
Hearst, William Randolph (newspaper magnate) 52
"Heathen Chinee,"42
Het Volk,(South African political party) 61
Ho Chi Minh, (Vietnamese nationalist) 67
Hong Kong, 7-9,18-20,22, 26-27,32,34,41,44,47-4863,65,66-67,91

Hong Kong-Canton Strike Boycott, 1925-1926 9, 65,87
Hong Kong-Canton Strike Committee,65
Hong Kong University, 26
Honolulu, 56
*Household Words,*34
Hudson,W.H (British naturalist),28
Hyde, Thomas(Bodley's Librarian) 16

I

India, 14-15,18,20,23,50,66,
Indian Mutiny, 20
Indian Ocean, 15
Industrial Revolution, 15,18
Iron Plough, 14
The Island of Paradise, 66

J

Jade, 21
Japan/Japanese 4,8-9, 13, 17,21,23,25-27,37, 44,47-48,50,52,56-57,63-64, 69-71
Jesuit, 8,15-16
"John Chinaman,"39,42
Journey to The West, 14

K

Kam Tin, 9,66
Katherine, Australia, 47
Korea, 8,13,15,23,27,50,67
Kowloon, 22,26,
Kropotkin, Peter, (Russian anarchist) 34

L

Lady Jocelyn, (ship) 39
Laquer, 14
Li Ta-chao (Chinese Communist) 63
Liao Tung Peninsula,48

Liberia 70
Limehouse,48,50-51
Lin Tse-hsu, (Chinese official) 18
Liverpool, 39,41-42,48,52
Liverpool Chinese Gospel Mission,42
London, 8-9 13,16,22,26-27,39-41,43-44,48,50-51,60,65,87,92
London, Jack, (author) 43,56-57
The London Magazine,July 1911, 41

M

Macartney, Lord George, (British diplomat),17
Mackenzie, John (author) 8,32
Mackerras,Colin (author) 34
Madagascar, 70
Mahatma Ghandi, (Indian activist) 61
Manchuria, 23,27,48
Mao and the Chinese Revolution, 64
Mao Tse-tung/Mao Zedong, (Chinese leader) 21,28,34,63
Marx, Karl, (economist and philosopher) 21
Mathematics, 15
May 30th Movement, 9, 64, 66
McKinley,President 37
Medicine, 15,17
Metallurgy, 8,14-15
Methodist Missionary Society, 8,26,
Michael, Archangel 37
Middle Kingdom, 15
The Middle Kingdom vol 1, 32,34,
Miller, Stuart Creighton (historian) 55
Ming Dynasty,14
Mozambique, 69
The Mystery of Fu Manchu, 48

N

Napoleon, 18
Nathan, Sir Matthew, (Hong Kong governor) 32
National Archives, Australia, 47

National Archives,London, 26,60,87
Navigation, 15
Needham, Joseph (Sinologist) 14
Nesbit E.(author) 44
New Territories, Hong Kong 8-9,47,66
The New York Times, August 18th 2007, 70
New Zealand, 44,47
Newspapers, National 9
Newspapers, Provincial 9
Nigeria 69
Ningpo, 19
Norman (Christian martyr) 27
North China Daily News 1926 or 1927, 63
North China Herald, 21

O

Occident,/Occidentalise, 13,25,31
Olympics,71, see also Beijing Olympics 2008
Opium/Opium Trade, 18-20,34,42,48,51,56
Opium War, First, 1841-1842, 17, 21, 32
Opium War, Second, 1856, 20-22, 32, 34
Opium, Smoking, 7, 18-19,39,40,43
Orient,31,
Orientalism,8,31-32,35,52
Orientalism, History, Theory and the Arts
Orientalism,(theory),8,31-32
Orientalist, 8
Overland China Mail February 21st 1905, 47
Overland China Mail July 30th 1925, 65,
Over The Water To China 44

P

Panikkar, K.M (author) 13
Peking, 15,17,20,21,26,27,42,63
Penarth Pier, Cardiff,39
Philippines,37
Polo, Marco, 15
Pope-Hennessy,Sir John (Hong Kong

governor) 8,22
Porcelain, 14,21,32,34
Port Arthur, 48
Port Holland, Australia, 47
Portuguese, 18,44
Protector (warship) 27-28

R

The Rand, 42,59-61
Red Guards, 66-67,
Red Peril, 53,65-66
Reformation, 14
Renaissance, 14
Rhodes House Library,Oxford,32
Rhubarb, 21
Riccii, Matteo(Jesuit) 15
Roath Basin, Cardiff,39,
Roath Dock,Cardiff 39
Robinson, (Christian martyr) 27
Rousseau, (philosopher) 21
Rupert G.G. (author) 50
Russia/Russian 13,18,20-21,23,25,47-48-50,57, 64,66,
Russo-Japanese War 1905, 9,21 48,

S

Said, Edward,(author) 8,23,28,31
San Francisco,56
Sax Rohmer, (author) 48
Scheffauer,Herman (author) 41
School of Oriental and African Studies, London,8,25-26
Science and Civilisation in China, 14
Scott Fitzgerald, F. (author) 52
Seamen, (in general),41
Seamen,British, 51
Seamen, Chinese, 9,41,51-52
Seamen, Liverpool, 52
Seamen,Welsh, 40
Seamen's Torch, 41
Seddon,Richard, (New Zealand prime minister) 44
Seed, Dr John,(British historian) 9,50,
Sewell, William Gawan, (author) 64
Shamchun, 27
Shameeen, 65
Shanghai 9,19,21,28,32,63-65,69,70
Shanghai Cotton Mill, 64
Shen, Fu Tsong (Chinese citizen)16
Sherlock Holmes,The Man With The Twisted Lip,43,
Shiel M.P. (author) 50
Sian/Xian,27, 28
Sierra Leone 70
Silk, 14,16,18,21,65
Singapore 7
Sino-Japanese War 1895, 8,23,27
South Africa,9,42,59,61,
South China Morning Post March 3rd 1908, 47,51
South China Morning Post August 27th 1908, 44,47
South China Morning Post May 27th 1925, 66
South Wales Daily News, 1908,40
South Wales Daily News, 1909,40
Solar Wind, 14
South China Sea, 15,18
South Korea, 71
Spence, Prof Jonathan, (Sinologist) 43-44,70
Sri Lanka, 15
Steel, 14,70
Stubbs,Sir Reginald (Hong Kong governor) 65-66
Sudan, 69
Sun Yat-sen,(Chinese nationalist) 26-27
Suspension bridge, 14
Swords,14

T

Tahiti, 47
Taiping Rebellion,42
Tales from The Yellow Emporium, 52

The Talons of Weng-Chiang, 51
Taku, 26-27
Tea, 14-16, 18,21
Temple, Robert, (author) 14
The Times December 26th 1869, 20
The Times January 7th 1905, 9
The Times December 20th 2004, 69
Tientsin, 27,
Tolstoy,Leo,(Russian author) 34
Townsville, Australia, 47
Treaty of Nanking, 1842 ,19
Treaty of Tientsin, 1858, 20,22
Treaty of Versailles,1919, 63
Tsingtao, 23,47
Tupper, (author and trade union leader) 39,41

U

U.S. Chinese Exclusion Act,1882 37
United States of America, 9,61,
The Unparalled Invasion, 57

V

The Valley of the Moon, 43,56
Victoria/Victorian 7,32,34,52

W

Wallace,Edgar (author) 50
Ward, Sir John (New Zealand premier) 47
Water Margin, 14
Wei-hai-wei, 7,48
Western Mail, July 22nd 1911, 40
Wilhelm, II Kaiser(German monarch) 37,57
Williams, Samuel Wells (author) 32
Wilson,President 63
World War One, 23, 63
World War Two, 56-57
Wyndham, Australia, 47

X

Xanadu, (poem) 7

Y

The Yellow Danger 50
The Yellow Peril or Orient vs Occident 50
The Yellow Snake 50

Z

Zambia, 69-70
Zanzibar, 15
Zheng He, 14-15
Zinc, 15
Zinoviev Letter, 65

W/e = Week ending

THE CENTRE FOR FORTEAN ZOOLOGY

So, what is the Centre for Fortean Zoology?

We are a non profit-making organisation founded in 1992 with the aim of being a clearing house for information, and coordinating research into mystery animals around the world. We also study out of place animals, rare and aberrant animal behaviour, and Zooform Phenomena; little-understood "things" that appear to be animals, but which are in fact nothing of the sort, and not even alive (at least in the way we understand the term).

Why should I join the Centre for Fortean Zoology?

Not only are we the biggest organisation of our type in the world, but - or so we like to think - we are the best. We are certainly the only truly global Cryptozoological research organisation, and we carry out our investigations using a strictly scientific set of guidelines. We are expanding all the time and looking to recruit new members to help us in our research into mysterious animals and strange creatures across the globe. Why should you join us? Because, if you are genuinely interested in trying to solve the last great mysteries of Mother Nature, there is nobody better than us with whom to do it.

What do I get if I join the Centre for Fortean Zoology?

For £12 a year, you get a four-issue subscription to our journal *Animals & Men*. Each issue contains 60 pages packed with news, articles, letters, research papers, field reports, and even a gossip column! The magazine is A5 in format with a full colour cover. You also have access to one of the world's largest collections of resource material dealing with cryptozoology and allied disciplines, and people from the CFZ membership regularly take part in fieldwork and expeditions around the world.

How is the Centre for Fortean Zoology organized?

The CFZ is managed by a three-man board of trustees, with a non-profit making trust registered with HM Government Stamp Office. The board of trustees is supported by a Permanent Directorate of full and part-time staff, and advised by a Consultancy Board of specialists - many of whom who are world-renowned experts in their particular field. We have regional representatives across the UK, the USA, and many other parts of the world, and are affiliated with other organisations whose aims and protocols mirror our own.

I am new to the subject, and although I am interested I have little practical knowledge. I don't want to feel out of my depth. What should I do?

Don't worry. We were *all* beginners once. You'll find that the people at the CFZ are friendly and approachable. We have a thriving forum on the website which is the hub of an ever-growing electronic community. You will soon find your feet. Many members of the CFZ Permanent Directorate started off as ordinary members, and now work full-time chasing monsters around the world.

I have an idea for a project which isn't on your website. What do I do?

Write to us, e-mail us, or telephone us. The list of future projects on the website is not exhaustive. If you have a good idea for an investigation, please tell us. We may well be able to help.

How do I go on an expedition?

We are always looking for volunteers to join us. If you see a project that interests you, do not hesitate to get in touch with us. Under certain circumstances we can help provide funding for your trip. If you look on the future projects section of the website, you can see some of the projects that we have pencilled in for the next few years.

In 2003 and 2004 we sent three-man expeditions to Sumatra looking for Orang-Pendek - a semi-legendary bipedal ape. The same three went to Mongolia in 2005. All three members started off merely subscribers to the CFZ magazine.

Next time it could be you!

Project Kerinci, Sumatra - 2003
In search of the bipedal ape Orang Pendek

How is the Centre for Fortean Zoology funded?

We have no magic sources of income. All our funds come from donations, membership fees, works that we do for TV, radio or magazines, and sales of our publications and merchandise. We are always looking for corporate sponsorship, and other sources of revenue. If you have any ideas for fund-raising please let us know. However, unlike other cryptozoological organisations in the past, we do not live in an intellectual ivory tower. We are not afraid to get our hands dirty, and furthermore we are not one of those organisations where the membership have to raise money so that a privileged few can go on expensive foreign trips. Our research teams both in the UK and abroad, consist of a mixture of experienced and inexperienced personnel. We are truly a community, and work on the premise that the benefits of CFZ membership are open to all.

What do you do with the data you gather from your investigations and expeditions?

Reports of our investigations are published on our website as soon as they are available. Preliminary reports are posted within days of the project finishing.

Each year we publish a 200 page yearbook containing research papers and expedition reports too long to be printed in the journal. We freely circulate our information to anybody who asks for it.

Is the CFZ community purely an electronic one?

No. Each year since 2000 we have held our annual convention - the *Weird Weekend* - in Exeter. It is three days of lectures, workshops, and excursions. But most importantly it is a chance for members of the CFZ to meet each other, and to talk with the members of the permanent directorate in a relaxed and informal setting and preferably with a pint of beer in one hand. Since 2006 - the *Weird Weekend* has been bigger and better and held in the idyllic rural location of Woolsery in North Devon. The 2008 event will be held over the weekend 15-17 August.

Since relocating to North Devon in 2005 we have become ever more closely involved with other community organisations, and we hope that this trend will continue. We also work closely with Police Forces across the UK as consultants for animal mutilation cases, and we intend to forge closer links with the coastguard and other community services. We want to work closely with those who regularly travel into the Bristol Channel, so that if the recent trend of exotic animal visitors to our coastal waters continues, we can be out there as soon as possible.

We are building a Visitor's Centre in rural North Devon. This will not be open to the general public, but will provide a museum, a library and an educational resource for our members (currently over 400) across the globe. We are also planning a youth organisation which will involve children and young people in our activities. We work closely with *Tropiquaria* - a small zoo in north Somerset, and have several exciting conservation projects planned.

Apart from having been the only Fortean Zoological organisation in the world to have consistently published material on all aspects of the subject for over a decade, we have achieved the following concrete results:

- Disproved the myth relating to the headless so-called sea-serpent carcass of Durgan beach in Cornwall 1975
- Disproved the story of the 1988 puma skull of Lustleigh Cleave
- Carried out the only in-depth research ever into the mythos of the Cornish Owlman
- Made the first records of a tropical species of lamprey
- Made the first records of a luminous cave gnat larva in Thailand.
- Discovered a possible new species of British mammal - the beech marten.
- In 1994-6 carried out the first archival fortean zoological survey of Hong Kong.
- In the year 2000, CFZ theories where confirmed when an entirely new species of lizard was found resident in Britain.
- Identified the monster of Martin Mere in Lancashire as a giant wels catfish
- Expanded the known range of Armitage's skink in the Gambia by 80%
- Obtained photographic evidence of the remains of Europe's largest known pike
- Carried out the first ever in-depth study of the *ninki-nanka*
- Carried out the first attempt to breed Puerto Rican cave snails in captivity
- Were the first European explorers to visit the `lost valley` in Sumatra
- Published the first ever evidence for a new tribe of pygmies in Guyana
- Published the first evidence for a new species of caiman in Guyana

EXPEDITIONS & INVESTIGATIONS TO DATE INCLUDE:

- 1998 Puerto Rico, Florida, Mexico *(Chupacabras)*
- 1999 Nevada *(Bigfoot)*
- 2000 Thailand *(Giant snakes called nagas)*
- 2002 Martin Mere *(Giant catfish)*
- 2002 Cleveland *(Wallaby mutilation)*
- 2003 Bolam Lake *(BHM Reports)*
- 2003 Sumatra *(Orang Pendek)*
- 2003 Texas *(Bigfoot; giant snapping turtles)*
- 2004 Sumatra *(Orang Pendek; cigau, a sabre-toothed cat)*
- 2004 Illinois *(Black panthers; cicada swarm)*
- 2004 Texas *(Mystery blue dog)*
- 2004 Puerto Rico *(Chupacabras; carnivorous cave snails)*
- 2005 Belize *(Affiliate expedition for hairy dwarfs)*
- 2005 Mongolia *(Allghoi Khorkhoi aka Mongolian death worm)*
- 2006 Gambia *(Gambo - Gambian sea monster , Ninki Nanka and Armitage s skink*
- 2006 Llangorse Lake *(Giant pike, giant eels)*
- 2006 Windermere *(Giant eels)*
- 2007 Coniston Water *(Giant eels)*
- 2007 Guyana *(Giant anaconda, didi, water tiger)*
- 2008 Russia *(Almasty)*

To apply for a <u>FREE</u> information pack about the organisation and details of how to join, plus information on current and future projects, expeditions and events.

Send a stamped and addressed envelope to:

**THE CENTRE FOR FORTEAN ZOOLOGY
MYRTLE COTTAGE, WOOLSERY,
BIDEFORD, NORTH DEVON
EX39 5QR.**

or alternatively visit our website at:
www.cfz.org.uk

Other books available from
CFZ PRESS

THE OWLMAN AND OTHERS - 30th Anniversary Edition
Jonathan Downes - ISBN 978-1-905723-02-7

£14.99

EASTER 1976 - Two young girls playing in the churchyard of Mawnan Old Church in southern Cornwall were frightened by what they described as a "nasty bird-man". A series of sightings that has continued to the present day. These grotesque and frightening episodes have fascinated researchers for three decades now, and one man has spent years collecting all the available evidence into a book. To mark the 30th anniversary of these sightings, Jonathan Downes has published a special edition of his book.

DRAGONS - More than a myth?
Richard Freeman - ISBN 0-9512872-9-X

£14.99

First scientific look at dragons since 1884. It looks at dragon legends worldwide, and examines modern sightings of dragon-like creatures, as well as some of the more esoteric theories surrounding dragonkind.

Dragons are discussed from a folkloric, historical and cryptozoological perspective, and Richard Freeman concludes that: "When your parents told you that dragons don't exist - they lied!"

MONSTER HUNTER
Jonathan Downes - ISBN 0-9512872-7-3

£14.99

Jonathan Downes' long-awaited autobiography, *Monster Hunter*...

Written with refreshing candour, it is the extraordinary story of an extraordinary life, in which the author crosses paths with wizards, rock stars, terrorists, and a bewildering array of mythical and not so mythical monsters, and still just about manages to emerge with his sanity intact.......

MONSTER OF THE MERE
Jonathan Downes - ISBN 0-9512872-2-2

£12.50

It all starts on Valentine's Day 2002 when a Lancashire newspaper announces that "Something" has been attacking swans at a nature reserve in Lancashire. Eyewitnesses have reported that a giant unknown creature has been dragging fully grown swans beneath the water at Martin Mere. An intrepid team from the Exeter based Centre for Fortean Zoology, led by the author, make two trips – each of a week – to the lake and its surrounding marshlands. During their investigations they uncover a thrilling and complex web of historical fact and fancy, quasi Fortean occurrences, strange animals and even human sacrifice.

CFZ PRESS, MYRTLE COTTAGE,
WOOLFARDISWORTHY BIDEFORD,
NORTH DEVON, EX39 5QR
w w w . c f z . o r g . u k

Other books available from
CFZ PRESS

ONLY FOOLS AND GOATSUCKERS
Jonathan Downes - ISBN 0-9512872-3-0

£12.50

In January and February 1998 Jonathan Downes and Graham Inglis of the Centre for Fortean Zoology spent three and a half weeks in Puerto Rico, Mexico and Florida, accompanied by a film crew from UK Channel 4 TV. Their aim was to make a documentary about the terrifying chupacabra - a vampiric creature that exists somewhere in the grey area between folklore and reality. This remarkable book tells the gripping, sometimes scary, and often hilariously funny story of how the boys from the CFZ did their best to subvert the medium of contemporary TV documentary making and actually do their job.

WHILE THE CAT'S AWAY
Chris Moiser - ISBN: 0-9512872-1-4

£7.99

Over the past thirty years or so there have been numerous sightings of large exotic cats, including black leopards, pumas and lynx, in the South West of England. Former Rhodesian soldier Sam McCall moved to North Devon and became a farmer and pub owner when Rhodesia became Zimbabwe in 1980. Over the years despite many of his pub regulars having seen the "Beast of Exmoor" Sam wasn't at all sure that it existed. Then a series of happenings made him change his mind. Chris Moiser—a zoologist—is well known for his research into the mystery cats of the westcountry. This is his first novel.

CFZ EXPEDITION REPORT 2006 - GAMBIA
ISBN 1905723032

£12.50

In July 2006, The J.T.Downes memorial Gambia Expedition - a six-person team - Chris Moiser, Richard Freeman, Chris Clarke, Oll Lewis, Lisa Dowley and Suzi Marsh went to the Gambia, West Africa. They went in search of a dragon-like creature, known to the natives as `Ninki Nanka`, which has terrorized the tiny African state for generations, and has reportedly killed people as recently as the 1990s. They also went to dig up part of a beach where an amateur naturalist claims to have buried the carcass of a mysterious fifteen foot sea monster named 'Gambo', and they sought to find the Armitage's Skink (*Chalcides armitagei*) - a tiny lizard first described in 1922 and only rediscovered in 1989. Here, for the first time, is their story.... With an forward by Dr. Karl Shuker and introduction by Jonathan Downes.

BIG CATS IN BRITAIN YEARBOOK 2006
Edited by Mark Fraser - ISBN 978-1905723-01-0

£10.00

Big cats are said to roam the British Isles and Ireland even now as you are sitting and reading this. People from all walks of life encounter these mysterious felines on a daily basis in every nook and cranny of these two countries. Most are jet-black, some are white, some are brown, in fact big cats of every description and colour are seen by some unsuspecting person while on his or her daily business. 'Big Cats in Britain' are the largest and most active group in the British Isles and Ireland This is their first book. It contains a run-down of every known big cat sighting in the UK during 2005, together with essays by various luminaries of the British big cat research community which place the phenomenon into scientific, cultural, and historical perspective.

**C F Z PRESS, MYRTLE COTTAGE,
WOOLSERY, BIDEFORD,
NORTH DEVON, EX39 5QR
w w w . c f z . o r g . u k**

Other books available from
CFZ PRESS

THE SMALLER MYSTERY CARNIVORES OF THE WESTCOUNTRY
Jonathan Downes - ISBN 978-1-905723-05-8

£7.99

Although much has been written in recent years about the mystery big cats which have been reported stalking Westcountry moorlands, little has been written on the subject of the smaller British mystery carnivores. This unique book redresses the balance and examines the current status in the Westcountry of three species thought to be extinct: the Wildcat, the Pine Marten and the Polecat, finding that the truth is far more exciting than the currently held scientific dogma. This book also uncovers evidence suggesting that even more exotic species of small mammal may lurk hitherto unsuspected in the countryside of Devon, Cornwall, Somerset and Dorset.

THE BLACKDOWN MYSTERY
Jonathan Downes - ISBN 978-1-905723-00-3

£7.99

Intrepid members of the CFZ are up to the challenge, and manage to entangle themselves thoroughly in the bizarre trappings of this case. This is the soft underbelly of ufology, rife with unsavoury characters, plenty of drugs and booze." That sums it up quite well, we think. A new edition of the classic 1999 book by legendary fortean author Jonathan Downes. In this remarkable book, Jon weaves a complex tale of conspiracy, anti-conspiracy, quasi-conspiracy and downright lies surrounding an air-crash and alleged UFO incident in Somerset during 1996. However the story is much stranger than that. This excellent and amusing book lifts the lid off much of contemporary forteana and explains far more than it initially promises.

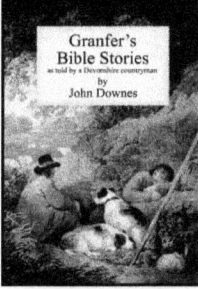

GRANFER'S BIBLE STORIES
John Downes - ISBN 0-9512872-8-1

£7.99

Bible stories in the Devonshire vernacular, each story being told by an old Devon Grandfather - 'Granfer'. These stories are now collected together in a remarkable book presenting selected parts of the Bible as one more-or-less continuous tale in short 'bite sized' stories intended for dipping into or even for bed-time reading. `Granfer` treats the biblical characters as if they were simple country folk living in the next village. Many of the stories are treated with a degree of bucolic humour and kindly irreverence, which not only gives the reader an opportunity to re-evaluate familiar tales in a new light, but do so in both an entertaining and a spiritually uplifting manner.

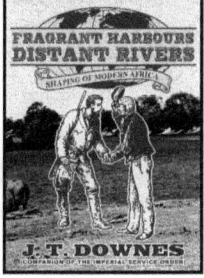

FRAGRANT HARBOURS DISTANT RIVERS
John Downes - ISBN 0-9512872-5-7

£12.50

Many excellent books have been written about Africa during the second half of the 19th Century, but this one is unique in that it presents the stories of a dozen different people, whose interlinked lives and achievements have as many nuances as any contemporary soap opera. It explains how the events in China and Hong Kong which surrounded the Opium Wars, intimately effected the events in Africa which take up the majority of this book. The author served in the Colonial Service in Nigeria and Hong Kong, during which he found himself following in the footsteps of one of the main characters in this book; Frederick Lugard – the architect of modern Nigeria.

CFZ PRESS, MYRTLE COTTAGE,
WOOLFARDISWORTHY BIDEFORD,
NORTH DEVON, EX39 5QR
w w w . c f z . o r g . u k

Other books available from
CFZ PRESS

ANIMALS & MEN - Issues 1 - 5 - In the Beginning
Edited by Jonathan Downes - ISBN 0-9512872-6-5

£12.50

At the beginning of the 21st Century monsters still roam the remote, and sometimes not so remote, corners of our planet. It is our job to search for them. The Centre for Fortean Zoology [CFZ] is the only professional, scientific and full-time organisation in the world dedicated to cryptozoology - the study of unknown animals. Since 1992 the CFZ has carried out an unparalleled programme of research and investigation all over the world. We have carried out expeditions to Sumatra (2003 and 2004), Mongolia (2005), Puerto Rico (1998 and 2004), Mexico (1998), Thailand (2000), Florida (1998), Nevada (1999 and 2003), Texas (2003 and 2004), and Illinois (2004). An introductory essay by Jonathan Downes, notes putting each issue into a historical perspective, and a history of the CFZ.

ANIMALS & MEN - Issues 6 - 10 - The Number of the Beast
Edited by Jonathan Downes - ISBN 978-1-905723-06-5

£12.50

At the beginning of the 21st Century monsters still roam the remote, and sometimes not so remote, corners of our planet. It is our job to search for them. The Centre for Fortean Zoology [CFZ] is the only professional, scientific and full-time organisation in the world dedicated to cryptozoology - the study of unknown animals. Since 1992 the CFZ has carried out an unparalleled programme of research and investigation all over the world. We have carried out expeditions to Sumatra (2003 and 2004), Mongolia (2005), Puerto Rico (1998 and 2004), Mexico (1998), Thailand (2000), Florida (1998), Nevada (1999 and 2003), Texas (2003 and 2004), and Illinois (2004). Preface by Mark North and an introductory essay by Jonathan Downes, notes putting each issue into a historical perspective, and a history of the CFZ.

BIG BIRD! Modern Sightings of Flying Monsters

Ken Gerhard - ISBN 978-1-905723-08-9

£7.99

From all over the dusty U.S./Mexican border come hair-raising stories of modern day encounters with winged monsters of immense size and terrifying appearance. Further field sightings of similar creatures are recorded from all around the globe. What lies behind these weird tales? Ken Gerhard is a native Texan, he lives in the homeland of the monster some call 'Big Bird'. Ken's scholarly work is the first of its kind. On the track of the monster, Ken uncovers cases of animal mutilations, attacks on humans and mounting evidence of a stunning zoological discovery ignored by mainstream science. Keep watching the skies!

STRENGTH THROUGH KOI
They saved Hitler's Koi and other stories

Jonathan Downes - ISBN 978-1-905723-04-1

£7.99

Strength through Koi is a book of short stories - some of them true, some of them less so - by noted cryptozoologist and raconteur Jonathan Downes. The stories are all about koi carp, and their interaction with bigfoot, UFOs, and Nazis. Even the late George Harrison makes an appearance. Very funny in parts, this book is highly recommended for anyone with even a passing interest in aquaculture, but should be taken definitely *cum grano salis*.

**CFZ PRESS, MYRTLE COTTAGE,
WOOLSERY, BIDEFORD,
NORTH DEVON, EX39 5QR**

Other books available from
CFZ PRESS

BIG CATS IN BRITAIN YEARBOOK 2007
Edited by Mark Fraser - ISBN 978-1-905723-09-6

£12.50

People from all walks of life encounter mysterious felids on a daily basis, in every nook and cranny of the UK. Most are jet-black, some are white, some are brown; big cats of every description and colour are seen by some unsuspecting person while on his or her daily business. 'Big Cats in Britain' are the largest and most active research group in the British Isles and Ireland. This book contains a run-down of every known big cat sighting in the UK during 2006, together with essays by various luminaries of the British big cat research community.

CAT FLAPS! Northern Mystery Cats
Andy Roberts - ISBN 978-1-905723-11-9

£6.99

Of all Britain`s mystery beasts, the alien big cats are the most renowned. In recent years the notoriety of these uncatchable, out-of-place predators have eclipsed even the Loch Ness Monster. They slink from the shadows to terrorise a community, and then, as often as not, vanish like ghosts. But now film, photographs, livestock kills, and paw prints show that we can no longer deny the existence of these once-legendary beasts. Here then is a case-study, a true lost classic of Fortean research by one of the country's most respected researchers.

CENTRE FOR FORTEAN ZOOLOGY 2007 YEARBOOK
Edited by Jonathan Downes and Richard Freeman
ISBN 978-1-905723-14-0

£12.50

The Centre For Fortean Zoology Yearbook is a collection of papers and essays too long and detailed for publication in the CFZ Journal *Animals & Men*. With contributions from both well-known researchers, and relative newcomers to the field, the Yearbook provides a forum where new theories can be expounded, and work on little-known cryptids discussed.

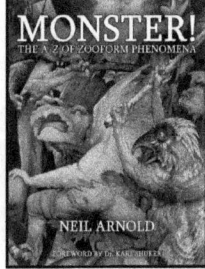

MONSTER! THE A-Z OF ZOOFORM PHENOMENA
Neil Arnold - ISBN 978-1-905723-10-2

£14.99

Zooform Phenomena are the most elusive, and least understood, mystery `animals`. Indeed, they are not animals at all, and are not even animate in the accepted terms of the word. Author and researcher Neil Arnold is to be commended for a groundbreaking piece of work, and has provided the world's first alphabetical listing of zooforms from around the world.

**CFZ PRESS, MYRTLE COTTAGE,
WOOLFARDISWORTHY BIDEFORD,
NORTH DEVON, EX39 5QR
w w w . c f z . o r g . u k**

Other books available from
CFZ PRESS

BIG CATS LOOSE IN BRITAIN
Marcus Matthews - ISBN 978-1-905723-12-6

£14.99

Big Cats: Loose in Britain, looks at the body of anecdotal evidence for such creatures: sightings, livestock kills, paw-prints and photographs, and seeks to determine underlying commonalities and threads of evidence. These two strands are repeatedly woven together into a highly readable, yet scientifically compelling, overview of the big cat phenomenon in Britain.

DARK DORSET
TALES OF MYSTERY, WONDER AND TERROR
Robert. J. Newland and Mark. J. North
ISBN 978-1-905723-15-6

£12.50

This extensively illustrated compendium has over 400 tales and references, making this book by far one of the best in its field. Dark Dorset has been thoroughly researched, and includes many new entries and up to date information never before published. The title of the book speaks for itself, and is indeed not for the faint hearted or those easily shocked.

MAN-MONKEY - IN SEARCH OF THE BRITISH BIGFOOT
Nick Redfern - ISBN 978-1-905723-16-4

£9.99

In her 1883 book, *Shropshire Folklore*, Charlotte S. Burne wrote: *'Just before he reached the canal bridge, a strange black creature with great white eyes sprang out of the plantation by the roadside and alighted on his horse's back'*. The creature duly became known as the `Man-Monkey`.

Between 1986 and early 2001, Nick Redfern delved deeply into the mystery of the strange creature of that dark stretch of canal. Now, published for the very first time, are Nick's original interview notes, his files and discoveries; as well as his theories pertaining to what lies at the heart of this diabolical legend.

EXTRAORDINARY ANIMALS REVISITED
Dr Karl Shuker - ISBN 978-1905723171

£14.99

This delightful book is the long-awaited, greatly-expanded new edition of one of Dr Karl Shuker's much-loved early volumes, *Extraordinary Animals Worldwide*. It is a fascinating celebration of what used to be called romantic natural history, examining a dazzling diversity of animal anomalies, creatures of cryptozoology, and all manner of other thought-provoking zoological revelations and continuing controversies down through the ages of wildlife discovery.

**CFZ PRESS, MYRTLE COTTAGE,
WOOLFARDISWORTHY BIDEFORD,
NORTH DEVON, EX39 5QR
w w w . c f z . o r g . u k**

Other books available from
CFZ PRESS

DARK DORSET CALENDAR CUSTOMS
Robert J Newland - ISBN 978-1-905723-18-8

£12.50

Much of the intrinsic charm of Dorset folklore is owed to the importance of folk customs. Today only a small amount of these curious and occasionally eccentric customs have survived, while those that still continue have, for many of us, lost their original significance. Why do we eat pancakes on Shrove Tuesday? Why do children dance around the maypole on May Day? Why do we carve pumpkin lanterns at Hallowe'en? All the answers are here! Robert has made an in-depth study of the Dorset country calendar identifying the major feast-days, holidays and celebrations when traditionally such folk customs are practiced.

CENTRE FOR FORTEAN ZOOLOGY 2004 YEARBOOK
Edited by Jonathan Downes and Richard Freeman
ISBN 978-1-905723-14-0

£12.50

The Centre For Fortean Zoology Yearbook is a collection of papers and essays too long and detailed for publication in the CFZ Journal *Animals & Men*. With contributions from both well-known researchers, and relative newcomers to the field, the Yearbook provides a forum where new theories can be expounded, and work on little-known cryptids discussed.

CENTRE FOR FORTEAN ZOOLOGY 2008 YEARBOOK
Edited by Jonathan Downes and Corinna Downes
ISBN 978 -1-905723-19-5

£12.50

The Centre For Fortean Zoology Yearbook is a collection of papers and essays too long and detailed for publication in the CFZ Journal *Animals & Men*. With contributions from both well-known researchers, and relative newcomers to the field, the Yearbook provides a forum where new theories can be expounded, and work on little-known cryptids discussed.

ETHNA'S JOURNAL
Corinna Newton Downes
ISBN 978 -1-905723-21-8

£9.99

Ethna's Journal tells the story of a few months in an alternate Dark Ages, seen through the eyes of Ethna, daughter of Lord Edric. She is an unsophisticated girl from the fortress town of Cragnuth, somewhere in the north of England, who reluctantly gets embroiled in a web of treachery, sorcery and bloody war...

**CFZ PRESS, MYRTLE COTTAGE,
WOOLFARDISWORTHY BIDEFORD,
NORTH DEVON, EX39 5QR
w w w . c f z . o r g . u k**

Other books available from
CFZ PRESS

ANIMALS & MEN - Issues 11 - 15 - The Call of the Wild
Jonathan Downes (Ed) - ISBN 978-1-905723-07-2

£12.50

Since 1994 we have been publishing the world's only dedicated cryptozoology magazine, *Animals & Men*. This volume contains fascimile reprints of issues 11 to 15 and includes articles covering out of place walruses, feathered dinosaurs, possible North American ground sloth survival, the theory of initial bipedalism, mystery whales, mitten crabs in Britain, Barbary lions, out of place animals in Germany, mystery pangolins, the barking beast of Bath, Yorkshire ABCs, Molly the singing oyster, singing mice, the dragons of Yorkshire, singing mice, the bigfoot murders, waspman, British beavers, the migo, Nessie, the weird warbling whatsit of the westcountry, the quagga project and much more...

IN THE WAKE OF BERNARD HEUVELMANS
Michael A Woodley - ISBN 978-1-905723-20-1

£9.99

Everyone is familiar with the nautical maps from the middle ages that were liberally festooned with images of exotic and monstrous animals, but the truth of the matter is that the *idea* of the sea monster is probably as old as humankind itself.

For two hundred years, scientists have been producing speculative classifications of sea serpents, attempting to place them within a zoological framework. This book looks at these successive classification models, and using a new formula produces a sea serpent classification for the 21st Century.

CENTRE FOR FORTEAN ZOOLOGY 1999 YEARBOOK
Edited by Jonathan Downes
ISBN 978 -1-905723-24-9

£12.50

The Centre For Fortean Zoology Yearbook is a collection of papers and essays too long and detailed for publication in the CFZ Journal *Animals & Men*. With contributions from both well-known researchers, and relative newcomers to the field, the Yearbook provides a forum where new theories can be expounded, and work on little-known cryptids discussed.

CENTRE FOR FORTEAN ZOOLOGY 1996 YEARBOOK
Edited by Jonathan Downes
ISBN 978 -1-905723-22-5

£12.50

The Centre For Fortean Zoology Yearbook is a collection of papers and essays too long and detailed for publication in the CFZ Journal *Animals & Men*. With contributions from both well-known researchers, and relative newcomers to the field, the Yearbook provides a forum where new theories can be expounded, and work on little-known cryptids discussed.

**CFZ PRESS, MYRTLE COTTAGE,
WOOLFARDISWORTHY BIDEFORD,
NORTH DEVON, EX39 5QR
w w w . c f z . o r g . u k**

Other books available from
CFZ PRESS

BIG CATS IN BRITAIN YEARBOOK 2008
Edited by Mark Fraser - ISBN 978-1-905723-23-2

£12.50

People from all walks of life encounter mysterious felids on a daily basis, in every nook and cranny of the UK. Most are jet-black, some are white, some are brown; big cats of every description and colour are seen by some unsuspecting person while on his or her daily business. 'Big Cats in Britain' are the largest and most active research group in the British Isles and Ireland. This book contains a run-down of every known big cat sighting in the UK during 2007, together with essays by various luminaries of the British big cat research community.

CFZ EXPEDITION REPORT 2007 - GUYANA
ISBN 978-1-905723-25-6

£12.50

Since 1992, the CFZ has carried out an unparalleled programme of research and investigation all over the world. In November 2007, a five-person team - Richard Freeman, Chris Clarke, Paul Rose, Lisa Dowley and Jon Hare went to Guyana, South America. They went in search of giant anacondas, the bigfoot-like didi, and the terrifying water tiger.

Here, for the first time, is their story...With an introduction by Jonathan Downes and forward by Dr. Karl Shuker.

CENTRE FOR FORTEAN ZOOLOGY 2003 YEARBOOK
Edited by Jonathan Downes and Richard Freeman
ISBN 978-1-905723-19-5

£12.50

The Centre For Fortean Zoology Yearbook is a collection of papers and essays too long and detailed for publication in the CFZ Journal *Animals & Men*. With contributions from both well-known researchers, and relative newcomers to the field, the Yearbook provides a forum where new theories can be expounded, and work on little-known cryptids discussed.

CENTRE FOR FORTEAN ZOOLOGY 1997 YEARBOOK
Edited by Jonathan Downes and Graham Inglis
ISBN 978-1-905723-27-0

£12.50

The Centre For Fortean Zoology Yearbook is a collection of papers and essays too long and detailed for publication in the CFZ Journal *Animals & Men*. With contributions from both well-known researchers, and relative newcomers to the field, the Yearbook provides a forum where new theories can be expounded, and work on little-known cryptids discussed.

**CFZ PRESS, MYRTLE COTTAGE,
WOOLFARDISWORTHY BIDEFORD,
NORTH DEVON, EX39 5QR
w w w . c f z . o r g . u k**

Other books available from
CFZ PRESS

CENTRE FOR FORTEAN ZOOLOGY 2000-1 YEARBOOK
Edited by Jonathan Downes and Richard Freeman
ISBN 978-1-905723-19-5

£12.50

The Centre For Fortean Zoology Yearbook is a collection of papers and essays too long and detailed for publication in the CFZ Journal *Animals & Men*. With contributions from both well-known researchers, and relative newcomers to the field, the Yearbook provides a forum where new theories can be expounded, and work on little-known cryptids discussed.

THE MYSTERY ANIMALS OF THE BRITISH ISLES: NORTHUMBERLAND AND TYNESIDE
Michael J Hallowell
ISBN 978-1-905723-29-4

£12.50

Mystery animals? Great Britain? Surely not. But is is true.

This is a major new series from CFZ Press. It will cover Great Britain and the Republic of Ireland, on a county by county basis, describing the mystery animals of the entire island group.

The Island of Paradise: Chupacabra, UFO Crash Retrievals, and Accelerated Evolution on the Island of Puerto Rico
Jonathan Downes - ISBN 978-1-905723-32-4

£14.99

In his first book of original research for four years, Jon Downes visits the Antillean island of Puerto Rico, to which he has led two expeditions - in 1998 and 2004. Together with noted researcher Nick Redfern he goes in search of the grotesque vampiric chupacabra, believing that it can - finally - be categorised within a zoological frame of reference rather than a purely paranormal one. Along the way he uncovers mystery after mystery, has a run in with terrorists, art historians, and even has his garden buzzed by a UFO. By turns both terrifying and funny, this remarkable book is a real tour de force by one of the world's foremost cryptozoological researchers.

DR SHUKER'S CASEBOOK
Dr Karl Shuker - ISBN 978-1905723-33-1

£14.99

Although he is best-known for his extensive cryptozoological researches and publications, Dr Karl Shuker has also investigated a very diverse range of other anomalies and unexplained phenomena, both in the literature and in the field. Now, compiled here for the very first time, are some of the extraordinary cases that he has re-examined or personally explored down through the years.

**CFZ PRESS, MYRTLE COTTAGE,
WOOLFARDISWORTHY BIDEFORD,
NORTH DEVON, EX39 5QR
w w w . c f z . o r g . u k**

Other books available from
CFZ PRESS

Dinosaurs and Other Prehistoric Animals on Stamps: A Worldwide Catalogue
Dr Karl P.N.Shuker - ISBN 978-1-905723-34-8

£9.99

Compiled by zoologist Dr Karl P.N. Shuker, a lifelong, enthusiastic collector of wildlife stamps and with an especial interest in those that portray fossil species, it provides an exhaustive, definitive listing of stamps and miniature sheets depicting dinosaurs and other prehistoric animals issued by countries throughout the world. It also includes sections dealing with cryptozoological stamps, dinosaur stamp superlatives, and unofficial prehistoric animal stamps.

CFZ EXPEDITION REPORT 2008 - RUSSIA
ISBN 978-1-905723-35-5

£12.50

Since 1992, the CFZ has carried out an unparalleled programme of research and investigation all over the world. In July 2008, a five-person team - Richard Freeman, Chris Clarke, Dave Archer, Adam Davies and Keith Townley went to Kabardino-Balkaria in southern Russia in search of the almasty, maybe mankind's closest relatives.

Here, for the first time, is their story...With an introduction by Jonathan Downes and forward by Dr. Karl Shuker.

CENTRE FOR FORTEAN ZOOLOGY 2009 YEARBOOK
Edited by Jonathan Downes and Richard Freeman
ISBN 978 -1-905723-37-9

£12.50

The Centre For Fortean Zoology Yearbook is a collection of papers and essays too long and detailed for publication in the CFZ Journal *Animals & Men*. With contributions from both well-known researchers, and relative newcomers to the field, the Yearbook provides a forum where new theories can be expounded, and work on little-known cryptids discussed.

THE MYSTERY ANIMALS OF THE BRITISH ISLES: KENT
Neil Arnold
ISBN 978-1-905723-36-2

£14.99

Mystery animals? Great Britain? Surely not. But is is true.

This is a major new series from CFZ Press. It will cover Great Britain and the Republic of Ireland, on a county by county basis, describing the mystery animals of the entire island group.

**CFZ PRESS, MYRTLE COTTAGE,
WOOLFARDISWORTHY BIDEFORD,
NORTH DEVON, EX39 5QR
w w w . c f z . o r g . u k**

Other books available from
CFZ PRESS

GIANT SNAKES
By Michael Newton
ISBN: 978-1-905723-30-0

£9.99

In this exciting book, Michael Newton takes an overview of the most terrifying uberpredators in the world - giant snakes. Outsized examples of known species as well as putative new species are looked at in detail. From fact to fiction, and from continent to continent, the stories and the science are examined, and the cryptozoological significance of these creatures explained. A fascinating (if slightly scary) book. Well done Michael.

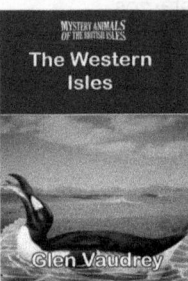

**THE MYSTERY ANIMALS OF THE BRITISH ISLES:
THE WESTERN ISLES**
Glen Vaudrey
ISBN 978-1-905723-42-3

£12.50

Mystery animals? Great Britain? Surely not. But is is true.

This is a major new series from CFZ Press. It will cover Great Britain and the Republic of Ireland, on a county by county basis, describing the mystery animals of the entire island group.

China: The Yellow Peril?
Richard Muirhead
ISBN 978-1-905723-41-6

£8.99

Richard Muirhead takes an in depth look at the history of Western relationships with China. If some Victorian antiquarians are to be believed contact between the Chinese Empire and other Middle Eastern and Western Empires goes back to times long before the birth of Christ, such as the ancient Egyptians and the Roman Empire. Muirhead`s book looks at a period of time long after these very early contacts, to the beginning of trading links between the West and China in the Seventeenth Century, with the arrival of the Jesuit intellectual and religious leaders, and continues to the present day.

CFZ PRESS, MYRTLE COTTAGE,
WOOLFARDISWORTHY BIDEFORD,
NORTH DEVON, EX39 5QR
w w w . c f z . o r g . u k

www.ingramcontent.com/pod-product-compliance
Lightning Source LLC
Chambersburg PA
CBHW070529100426
42743CB00010B/2005